The Home Stretch

The Home Stretch:

from prison to parole

Erwin James

Atlantic Books
London

For Margaret, whose love and loyalty helped to
transform my life, inside and out.

First published in 2005 by Atlantic Books, on behalf of Guardian Newspapers
Ltd. Atlantic Books is an imprint of Grove Atlantic Ltd.

10 9 8 7 6 5 4 3 2 1

A CIP catalogue record for this book is available from the British Library.

ISBN 1 84354 438 5

Printed in Great Britain by Mackays of Chatham, Chatham, Kent
Design by Helen Ewing

Atlantic Books
An Imprint of Grove Atlantic Ltd
Ormond House
26–27 Boswell Street
London
WC1N 3JZ

Contents

Introduction

Erwin James

The pen hadn't changed. It had the same cracked and weed-strewn tarmac surface that I remembered, enclosed on one side by a red-brick wall and on the other three sides and the top by the same rigid galvanized steel meshing that I could never forget. I'd only been out for a week when I found myself back inside the big London prison where my life sentence had begun twenty years earlier. I hadn't expected to see the pen ever again, but this time I was back in for a good reason. As a result of my writing for the *Guardian* I'd been invited in to sit on an advisory committee for a major arts project that the prison was hosting. The fact that it had been my first place of confinement all those years before was pure coincidence. When the meeting was over I spoke to the prison Governor who had chaired the meeting and told him about this odd turn of fate. 'Amazing when you think about it,' I said. The Governor, the ninth incumbent since the beginning of my life inside pursed his lips and nodded. 'I'd never have guessed,' he said, 'but if you're up for it, I'd be happy to give you a tour of the place.'

It was an offer I couldn't refuse, a unique chance to survey my beginnings on this formidable journey and get a real measure of the distance I had since travelled. The Governor led off and after traipsing through vaguely familiar corridors and wings, passing groups of unlocked prisoners chatting outside cell doors, and being introduced to the occasional member of staff, we arrived at my old wing. My cell had been on the top landing in a section that was known as A Seg. In those days half the landing was blocked off to create a segregated unit for high-security Category A prisoners, of whom I was one. There were twenty cells in the unit then, but no more than half were ever occupied at any one time. Now the segregated portion of the wing had been opened up and the partition walls removed. Prisoners hung over the railings peering down at me looking up. I searched for what would have been my old cell door, until my eyes rested upon it at the end of the landing. 'Do you want to go up and have a look?' asked the Governor when I pointed it out to him. 'No thanks,' I said, though I was tempted. The year I'd spent behind that door on twenty-three-hour bang-up ('bang-up' is the time prisoners spend locked in their cells) was probably the most intense period of my entire life. Nineteen years after I'd vacated it the image of what the interior of the cell had looked like hadn't left me. I didn't need to see it again. But I wondered if the pen where we had been allowed to spend the other hour of each day out in the fresh air still existed. 'Oh yes,' said the Governor. 'Come with me.'

I followed him down some more stairs and through another couple of steel gates, along another corridor and finally out through a heavy wooden door that led into the prison yards. While he locked the door behind us I stared up and around at the great cliff walls of the wings and the row after row of heavily barred cell windows, a life behind every one.

'Bring back memories?' said the Governor, smiling. I widened my eyes and nodded. On we walked until, after rounding another couple of corners, the pen burst into view and stopped me in my tracks. 'Christ,' I said. I'd never seen it from the outside. Much to my relief it was empty. 'We only use it now for the people with mental-health problems on D Wing,' said the Governor, 'and they don't come out very often.'

Even in my day the pen had never been a busy place. For security reasons only a maximum of two or three of us from A Seg had been allowed in it at any one time. For thirty minutes of my daily hour I used to walk around in circles. For the rest of the time I'd crouch in the far corner with my back against the wall and think about what might lie ahead of me and wonder how I was going to handle it.

When the Governor unlocked the gate into the pen and held it open for me I walked right in without hesitation. Moments later I was standing on the spot where a lifetime earlier I'd spent so many half hours in uncertain contemplation. Without warning, ghosts of the men who had once shared that yard with me drifted into view, the same men who like me had faced spending the prime years of their lives incarcerated. We had all been so young then, not one of us over thirty.

Of course I wouldn't have said it at the time, but going to prison for life turned out to be the best thing that ever happened to me. It brought to an end a life outside that had appeared to be without purpose for as long as I could remember. From an early age I'd been constantly on the move from one unhappy place to another. A prison psychologist once described my formative years as 'brutal and rootless', a perfect summing up I thought. My adolescence and early adulthood brought no discernible improvement and my behaviour became increasingly antisocial. By the time I entered the prison system for an indeterminate term, therefore, there seemed little prospect that anything good would come from my incarceration. My visit back to the pen reminded me of how hopeless my situation had looked at that time. I never imagined then that prison would end up transforming my life for the better as much as it did.

'All right?' asked the Governor. He'd been standing watching me from the open gate.

'Yes,' I said. 'I'm fine. Thanks for this.'

'You're welcome.'

The Governor escorted me back through his maze of steel and concrete and we said our farewells at the gatehouse. It felt good to walk out of there, but I was surprised at how painless it had been to see the place from the inside again. The short time I'd spent in the pen was surreal, but somehow uplifting. It reminded me of how far away I was from the young man who'd crouched in a state of such grave uncertainty against its red-brick wall – so far that we'd never have recognized each other.

I had just begun my sixteenth year of imprisonment when the opportunity to write for the *Guardian* presented itself. The previous years had not been wasted, however. Once I had adapted to the basic hostility of the prison environment, with some guidance from several well-disposed members of prison staff, I found I was able to look beyond immediate survival and begin to reap some tangible benefits. The same psychologist who described my childhood so succinctly encouraged me to attend education classes. Exercising my brain in such a way was a new experience. I discovered that the more effort I put into trying to achieve something, the more likely I was to succeed. This knowledge enabled me to develop a whole new attitude. I'd always had it in the back of my mind that there had to be more to me than I'd become on the outside, but I could never see a way to find out if that was true. Education – first evening classes and then an Open University degree course – provided me with the means. For most of my life I'd harboured profound feelings of inferiority. I'd been inarticulate and socially inhibited to the point of disablement. It took me ten years of life in prison to develop a character that I believed was almost the converse and that I was confident was authentic. By the time I got to my sixteenth year though I was flagging. For, no matter how resourceful a person may be, there is only so much that can be done in a penal institution to make a life feel meaningful. The more I'd grown, the more frustrating the constraints of prison life had become.

Writing *A Life Inside* gave me a new sense of purpose. It allowed me to engage with the outside world in a way that I'd never have thought was possible without first being released. Writing for readers of a national newspaper was in itself a form of release. The column gave me all the motivation I needed to maintain an optimistic outlook. It was a chance to put my new abilities to real practical use. Communicating with editors, negotiating with prison authorities to get their approval for the column to go ahead, knuckling down to produce copy that was good enough to appear in one of the most respected newspapers in the world: this was a challenge like no other I'd ever encountered. It helped that I started to think of myself not as a prisoner writing, but as a writer in prison. Suddenly, from being a powerless captive, I became an active observer, a chronicler of secret lives lived out in dark places.

But not everyone thought it was a good thing. The first governor I'd spoken to when trying to get official approval for the undertaking had been adamant that I would never be allowed to write for the *Guardian* under any circumstances. 'Read my lips,' he'd said. 'No prisoner is allowed to contact the media.' Thanks to the tenacity of the *Guardian's* G2 editor Ian Katz, whose patient negotiations with the upper echelons of the prison service hierarchy finally led to the prisons' minister announcing that he was 'content' for our groundbreaking project to happen, that governor was very pleasingly proved wrong. But I wasn't out to make enemies. I just kept out of his way once the column started appearing in the paper. It was the same with the assistant governor who gave a memorable response to my argument that allowing a prisoner to write for a major newspaper from his prison cell was actually a sign of a healthy society. 'It might help people who are interested to understand a bit more about this mysterious way of life,' I said. 'Your approval would signal that you and your colleagues really do believe in the concept of rehabilitation.' Leaning over his desk and looking directly at me through his rimless glasses he said, 'I could give you one big no... or fifty small no's. But the answer would still be the same I'm afraid.'

Even after official sanctioning, obstacles remained. Yet another governor, feigning support, summoned me to his office one day. He congratulated me on getting a result and asked if there was any way he could help. 'I know,' he said, 'when you've written your article, give it me to and I'll check through it and then post it on for you.' Stifling a combination of a grimace and a snigger I managed to politely decline his dubious offer. 'Thanks,' I said, 'but no thanks.'

Getting the copy to the copytakers was an adventure in itself. First I'd write the column in longhand, usually over three or four long nights of bang-up. (A kind, cigar-smoking PO – Principal Officer – who turned out to be a secret *Guardian* reader was supportive and made sure I always had a plentiful supply of A4 paper.

'Just make sure I get a mention' he implored.) Ian Katz sent money for me to buy phonecards so that I could telephone the copytakers. When the column was ready I'd charge round to join the phone queue as soon as the cell doors were opened for evening association. There were funny looks from my fellow cons as I dictated my copy down the telephone to an often bemused sounding copytaker. Especially when I was reporting particularly sensitive goings on, like escape plans for example or drug-dealing ventures, and I had to lower my voice to barely a whisper. More than once a copytaker had asked me, 'Are you a real prisoner? In prison?'

'Er, yes I am,' I'd say bashfully, willing his or her fingers to tap tap tap faster in order to preserve phonecard units, and save my blushes.

One time I was dictating copy from the telephone on the hospital wing. A column usually took three twenty-unit phonecards to dictate – two and a half if the copytaker was particularly fast. On this occasion the copytaker was inordinately slow, and was suffering from a merciless cough. During every other sentence I was having to pause while my typist reacted to her irritated throat. 'I'm down to my last phonecard,' I said. 'Please can we go a bit quicker.' As the woman exploded into a fresh bout of raucous spluttering the door leading to the alcove where the phone was located burst open and in dived a man who had escaped from a hospital cell, immediately followed by four prison officers and a 'nurse' (a prison officer with a nursing qualification wearing a white cotton tunic) wielding a large hypodermic syringe. The man was brought down screaming right by my feet. 'Got the bastard!' one of the officers shouted. The man screamed again. 'I got him too!' shouted the nurse, waving his empty syringe triumphantly, before the man was dragged back through the door. 'I don't suppose you got that?' I queried down the phone facetiously when the alcove was at peace again. 'Sorry, I was coughing,' the woman said. 'I missed it. Could you say it again please?' As I spoke the last few words of the final sentence the machine spat out the phonecard, indicating five seconds left.

It was the closest I ever got to missing a deadline. 'That's it,' I said, just before the line went dead. 'End copy.'

I wrote the column from the confines of a closed prison for almost two years. During that time I discovered that writing is no easy profession. While some pieces did seem to run easily from the end of my pen, sometimes taking no more than two or three hours to complete, the majority took up to ten hours and longer. Coming up with ideas was almost as painful. My day jobs in the prison included working as a wing cleaner, as a hand in the timber workshop, as the hospital orderly, and lastly as the reception orderly. I never missed the hour we were allowed to take each day in the exercise yard and used the gym usually three or four times a week. Being so actively involved in prison life meant that I always had a good overview of what was going on in the place, who was doing what, and to whom – although really that was nothing new. I found out many years earlier that the more a prisoner knows about his environment and its inhabitants the safer he is. I'd learned to keep my eyes and ears open at all times. All that had changed was that I was now putting this valuable aspect of how I did my time to another good use. But even then stories interesting enough to report and which gave some insights into our mostly secret existence were often hard to find. In the main my fellow prisoners were ignorant to the full extent of my writing activities. I had to remain discreet. Since my brother cons formed the core of my material I had to ensure that I protected their identities, which I did by changing names, timescales and locations.

Another reason I couldn't broadcast what I was doing was for fear of arousing suspicion, or resentment – being a 'tall poppy' in jail is a sure way of inviting attack. If the column was going to have some duration I couldn't afford to be ex-communicated and see the free flow of information drying up. The only fellow prisoners I trusted in the beginning were two other long termers, one of whom I'd known since almost the start of my sentence. They were men who did their own time, held their own counsel and relied on their own resources to get them through their days inside. In the column I gave them new names, Big Rinty and Felix the Gambler, and whenever I was really stuck for something to write about they never failed to offer to share their wisdom. We'd meet in Rinty's cell for emergency brainstorming sessions, the results of which were usually enough to give me a lead on a story and get my creative juices flowing. Thinking about it now I'm not sure that I would have been able to sustain the column without their input. Thanks again friends. (At the time of writing Big Rinty has served twenty-five years and is still in a closed prison. Felix has served eighteen years and is being let out daily from his open prison to work in a local recycling plant. The signs are that he will be released in 2005.)

Filing the column became a lot easier once I got downgraded to D Category status and began writing it from open conditions. For one, the phones were in booths so it was no longer necessary to stand in a prison-landing queue and dictate my copy in public view. And since we were never locked in our rooms I could choose the quietest times to use the phone. When I started working outside the prison I'd file my copy from public phone kiosks. Later, because the prison was close to London, I was allowed to visit the *Guardian* offices and sit and write my column on the features desk for one day each week. Sitting among writers whom I'd long admired was like being a fan of a popular soap opera who had fulfilled an impossible dream and joined the cast. Despite the fact that it must have been at the very least mildly unsettling for some *Guardian* staff to have a serving prisoner sitting alongside them, let alone one doing life, never once was I made aware of any unease, or unhappiness about my presence. Not a single person made me feel unwelcome. To everybody at 119 Farringdon Road, for that courtesy, thank you all.

The columns in this book recount my experiences and observations over the last year and a half of my life sentence as I emerged gradually back into the outside world. At first it seemed like a different world to the one I'd been effectively cocooned from since 1984. With the ending of the cold war, the fall of the

Berlin Wall, the freeing and presidential election of Nelson Mandela and more recently the September 11th attack on the Twin Towers, the state of the world had altered dramatically while I'd been away. But apart from technological advances (mobile phones, cash machines, multi–multi-channel television, the Internet), new coinage (£2 coins, 20p pieces) and a New Labour government, once I'd focused properly I came to the conclusion that these did not really amount to a major change. People were still the same, still harbouring the same worries, the same hopes, the same fears (though the latter had been heightened due to the relatively new 'war on terror'). And, just like through the ages, everybody's biggest concern is trying to get by in their day-to-day lives as best they can. The only real change that I can attest to unequivocally is the change for the better that those twenty years in prison enabled within me. I owed that much to the people I harmed. In the end 'life' gave me a new life. Now all I want to do is live it in a proper manner. I'm grateful that I live in a society that will allow that.

February 2005

Homeless but not that hungry

'Homeless and hungry.' That's what the cardboard sign hanging around the young man's neck said in large black letters. He was hunkered down in the shop doorway with an old blanket around his knees, part of which also covered his sleeping dog. It was dark and it was raining and I was walking from work to the station to catch my train back to the prison. It wasn't the first time I'd seen him, but it was the first time I'd seen him with a sign. I wondered what had changed. On previous occasions his appearance alone had been enough to let passers-by work out his circumstances for themselves. Only he knew how effective this was in securing donations, though his sign was perhaps a clue that the message had not been getting across as effectively as he would have liked.

Seeing 'homeless people' had been a shock when I first start-ed coming out of prison. I remember my first 'escorted town visit' at my last jail with my case officer at the time, Mr Turnlock. We were walking through a shopping centre when I heard a voice call out above the bustle, 'Any spare change friend?' I looked down and a man not long out of his twenties was smil-ing up at me from beside an overflowing wheelie bin. The skin on his face was taut and pock-marked and his long hair was greasy and lank. It was a warm midsummer morning but he was wearing several layers of clothes. They were probably all he had and I imagined he would be reluctant to take any off, no matter how high the temperature rose.

I had £50 in my pocket, money I had saved from my prison wages especially for this shopping trip. I'd been given instructions to buy goodies for my pals (Big Rinty wanted a giant-size Milky Bar, Felix the Gambler wanted 'original pear drops, not imita-tions'), otherwise the rest of the money was for me to buy civil-ian clothes with. I hoped it would stretch to a couple of decent shirts, maybe some socks. But when I saw the young man look-ing so broken I had an urge to stick my hand in my pocket and

1

ERWIN JAMES

hand over the five new tenners. Mr Turnlock saw me hesitate and said, 'C'mon, don't let him bother you.'

'I was just going to give him something,' I said, 'but I haven't got any change.'

'Don't be fooled by that "poor me" look,' said Mr Turnlock. 'They make fucking fortunes at that game.'

I doubted it somehow. Not the vast majority anyway. I wanted to talk to this young man and ask him what had happened. He looked dejected, but I could still see life in his eyes. I remembered times in my own life when I'd been down and out. In jail I had worked out that to an extent much of what we think of as our 'lot' we inflict on ourselves. Believing that I was a loser made it almost inevitable that I would lose. That was my theory anyway. I didn't think I could change this young man's situation. In fact, I'd no idea what my intentions were. There was just something so incongruous about me, a prisoner, being well fed, well shod and standing out in the sunshine with money in my pocket, while this man sat dressed in rags, holding out his hand and saying 'Please'. To Mr Turnlock's credit he reached into his trouser pocket and pulled out a pound coin. 'Here,' he said, and placed it in the man's outstretched hand before urging me on. It's hard to believe that encounter took place barely eighteen months ago.

I'd given the man with the dog money before – loose change only, no more than twenty or thirty pence at a time. I couldn't afford any more when I was on unpaid work. This time I had no change, just a £5 note. But I had half my prison sandwiches left, supplied by cook in lieu of meals for all those who 'work out'; corned beef or Spam is the usual filling, but they are free and provide the necessary fuel for a day's work. I usually eat half during the day and save the other half for my supper. But on this occasion the man in the doorway looked like his need for some supper was greater than mine.

I reached over the dog and said, 'You're welcome to these, mate.' His arm shot out and his hand grasped the clingfilm-wrapped package. I don't know what he expected but the

2

expression on his face changed in seconds from humble acceptance to puzzlement and then to fury. Before I could explain what
the package contained, he'd launched it back at me yelling, 'I
don't want your fuckin' sandwiches!'

It served me right I suppose, for making assumptions. I
managed to stop myself from apologizing – he was, after all,
advertising his hunger. But I was embarrassed, a feeling that was
intensified when his outburst attracted the attention of other
passers-by. I backed away awkwardly and continued to the station
with a brisker stride. Once I'd put some distance between us
I comforted myself with some humorous thoughts. 'Good job
I didn't tell him they were prison sandwiches... I'm sure the
dog would have welcomed the chance to offer a second
opinion.' I smiled to myself, but I was still uneasy about the man's
predicament. Later, warm and safe on the train, I really wished I'd
offered him the fiver instead.

16 January 2003

Tam the Man gives the governor short shrift

The end came suddenly for Tam the Man. It was only the other
week that he was telling a group of us gathered in his room about
his prospects for promotion at work. He'd started with the contract maintenance company (after 104 other job applications) less
than four months earlier, yet already he had proved himself
sufficiently well motivated for the manager to make plans to
enrol him on a series of development courses. 'They think I'll
make a good ganger,' he explained.

It figured. Not that Tam is a bossy man. On the contrary, he is
witty and his forthright way of communicating endeared him to
people on the landings – that and his uncomplaining attitude,
which served as a sobering example to others. (After completing
eleven years of his life sentence Tam was released, only to be
recalled some time later for buying a couple of pairs of jeans

'from a man in a pub' that turned out to have been stolen. This act of folly cost him another ten years in prison – an unimaginable ordeal to people serving fixed sentences, whose hearts in the main are constantly beating for the gate.)

His openness made him trusted by the majority of his fellow prisoners, which was why he often had a roomful during association time on his days off. Not all those present would necessarily get on together away from Tam's company. But he had that rare gift – rarer still in prison – of being able to bring people together. That's what his boss must have recognized.

Tam showed his true character when he prepared the way for two fellow prisoners to get jobs with his company. He got the men interviews on the strength of his recommendations – appraisals that were obviously accurate, as they both got immediate starts. The company had never even interviewed a prisoner before Tam, let alone employed one. Yet now they're looking at the prison as a source of reliable labour.

Nevertheless, Tam's unambiguous manner sometimes caused him problems with the prison authorities. He was never a 'yes man' – another reason for his popularity. But I feel this must have contributed to his having had to serve all those extra years. As unreasonable as this seems, there appears to be no other explanation.

A governor brought the news to Tam on Friday morning. He was just off a night shift spent out in the cold and had barely taken off his fluorescent jacket. It had been a wild, wet night and all he was thinking about was a shower and his bed, when the governor tapped on his room door.

'Come in,' called Tam. The governor had recently returned from a holiday abroad. Tam couldn't help noticing how fit and tanned he looked and made a complimentary remark. 'Thank you,' said the governor, and proceeded to describe his wonderful holiday in great detail until Tam's patience wore thin.

'Look, governor,' he said, 'no disrespect, but I'm just about to get my head down. Is there any special reason you want to see me?'

'Oh sorry, yes, there is,' said the governor. 'We've just been notified by head office. You're to be released on Monday.'

All credit to Tam. He gave the governor a long look and then shooed him out of the room. 'Please. Out you go,' he said, adding, 'I really have got to get my head down,' before closing the door on the startled bearer of good news.

I'd say that was a pretty cool response after twenty-one years in jail. But I'm still puzzled as to why Tam had to spend so long inside. If it was punishment it was misguided, as anyone who knows anything about these things knows that prison as punishment loses its impact if people are kept in too long. Deterrence perhaps? Well, the magistrate who sentenced him for receiving the dodgy jeans thought the offence was worth just four months' imprisonment, of which a 'normal' offender would spend only two in custody. I doubt that he envisaged it would be another nine years and two months before Tam would be allowed to rejoin society.

Actually I think I know the answer. The truth is that it's just the way the lifer system works, or doesn't work, sometimes. Some people turn into 'grey men' and seem to get forgotten about, others receive knock-backs on their parole applications for not displaying the 'right attitude' during call-ups for reports. Whatever it was in Tam's case, as far as I can see, all that was achieved by keeping him in for so long was that society was unnecessarily denied the services of an able contributor.

23 January 2003

The trauma of innocence

There have been days during my gradual reintroduction to society when I have found myself overwhelmed. The train journey which left me drenched in sweat after forty minutes of such intense self-consciousness that at one stage I thought I was going to have an out-of-body experience; the time I hovered for half an hour outside a barber's shop desperate for my first civilized haircut in nearly eighteen years, but ultimately too nervous to enter for fear of being unable to manage friendly chit-chat convincingly; and the encounter with the pretty checkout girl who smiled and wished me a good day when I paid for a bag of crisps, making me want to cry as I walked away. I don't like to admit it, but it has been at the end of days like these when I've been thankful to return to the familiar territory of my prison room.

It's comforting to know also that on 'days in', if the need arises, I can always speak to my case officer, who will offer reassurance and guidance about difficulties I might be encountering as I adjust to the outside world. (Lifers are allowed a maximum of five days out per week, which means an obligatory two 'days in', while fixed-termers can get six days out.) If problems persist, there is even a dedicated counsellor. And if I want to open a bank account or contact housing officials, or if I have need of social services, the 'throughcare' department will assist. There's no doubt that when it comes to releasing a long-term prisoner the prison authorities have an adequate system in place. But this is not the case for victims of miscarriages of justice.

Prior to this week, apart from the provision of financial compensation, which incidentally can often take years to come through, there was no such help for those wrongly convicted by the courts and then released, sometimes ten, fifteen, or even twenty or more years later. (Most prisoners 'in denial' are refused places on 'pre-release' courses and are not even considered for acclimatization activities such as escorted shopping trips or supervised work in the community.) But on Monday a new scheme was launched to provide support and advice for people who are to be released after suffering wrongful imprisonment.

The Home Office-funded scheme involves staff from Citizens' Advice Bureaus making arrangements to ensure that the people affected have access to counsellors and are given whatever advice is needed, including how to go about claiming compensation. It seems incredible, given the steady stream of damaged people who have been emerging from British prisons during the past twenty years or so, that such a scheme has not been organized before now.

Not that it was something I had spent much time thinking about before my own release plan began. But once I'd learned to anticipate and deal with my little panics, I got to wondering how the wrongfully convicted manage to cope when they are released so suddenly and with no such safety net.

Like the man on the television news one night, for example, who kissed the ground outside the Court of Appeal following the quashing of his conviction after sixteen years. He had been a boy of sixteen when his ordeal began. I knew him in the adult system, lived on the same landings with him, saw his pleading and protests first hand – and, along with everybody else who came into contact with him, witnessed his mental deterioration as the years passed. He must have thought his problems were over when he was kissing the ground, but I'd guess that, once he was back on his feet and the adrenalin had stopped pumping, it would prove to be little more than the beginning of a new ordeal.

Or the twenty-one-year-old I worked alongside in a prison workshop years earlier. He was innocent, 'really innocent', he'd tell me and others, over and over again. 'The truth will come out soon,' he told us. 'My mum won't let them keep me in when she knows I shouldn't be here.' We used to smile behind his back at that one. Fifteen years later I opened a newspaper one morning and there he was, prematurely aged and grey-haired, standing outside the Court of Appeal next to a proud-looking, elegantly dressed woman, identified as his mother. He had been cleared. Thank goodness for mothers, I remember thinking.

I've known many like my two former acquaintances and no doubt there will be many more to come. But at least now there will be help waiting when the gates finally open – and not before time. A society that caters so commendably for the guilty should not have to think twice about supporting the innocent.

30 January 2003

Wheeler's new wheels

Stepping briskly along the landings, striding purposefully into the dining room, or marching around the grounds in his free time – wherever Wheeler went it appeared that he had to get there fast. When he first landed here, the speculators thought it meant that he hadn't been inside for very long. But no, it turned out that he was doing a lump – a six-year stretch – and he had already done three. The weeks passed and Wheeler's pace persisted.

Somebody who had done time with him in the closed system said he had always been the same. 'The geezer never stops,' said the person in the know. 'We used to call him the Roadrunner.' On the out, we learned, Wheeler had been a semi-professional racing-car driver. The story was that it had been his swift attempt to secure funds for his racing team that had landed him in prison.

My first conversation with Wheeler took place in the prison library. It was an easy Sunday morning and the newspapers had just arrived. While other prisoners sat around, languidly perusing the latest scandals and controversies, Wheeler stood at the counter, rapidly turning the pages of one of the broadsheets. When it looked like he had finished, I asked him if I could take the paper. 'Sure,' he replied, 'I only read the headlines.'

He seemed friendly enough, so I said, 'You always seem to be in such a hurry. Don't you ever relax?' Close up, his facial skin was stretched tight and I couldn't help noticing that his fingernails were bitten down to the quick.

'Relax?' he said, as if I had unexpectedly poked him in the eye. 'No time to relax,' he added, before turning and showing me a clean pair of heels.

Once I had started going out to work, I found that it was possible to go two or three weeks without bumping into individual fellow prisoners. When I was in, I would occasionally see Wheeler's head and shoulders darting past a window, or I would catch his back as he disappeared into the education block or the gym. But I never saw him again to speak to until one evening, a few weeks ago, when I got off the train after the journey back from work. The prison van was waiting as usual. I climbed in the back and heard a voice I didn't recognize at first call from the driver's cab, 'Evenin'.'

'Evenin',' I replied, unable to conceal the surprise in my voice. It was Wheeler. Surprise? On reflection, I think it was alarm.

There were three other passengers already in the van. Remarkably, all had fastened their seatbelts. Naturally, I fastened mine. Since I was the last man on the list to be collected for at least another hour, Wheeler started the van and pulled away.

I have never been on a real roller-coaster, but that night, twisting and turning at high speeds on unlit country back roads, Wheeler gave me a flavour of what it must be like. Rocking to one side of the seat, rolling to the other – to a brave fly on one of the van's walls, the four of us in the back would have looked like we were doing some sort of formation passenger routine. Eight minutes later, the van screeched to a halt in the prison car park and the four of us made an urgent exit, grateful and relieved to get our feet back on solid ground.

Of course, there was no acknowledgement that any of us had been spooked. Even in 'open conditions' it is unwise to show fear in prison. Which meant that we were probably going to be at the mercy of Wheeler's fast-wheeling until he, too, was eligible for paid work, or until he wrote off the van – preferably with none of us in it.

There were plenty of whispers, however, which grew louder with each nerve-wracking journey – and, I suspect, an anonymous note or three in the wing postbox. But with the prison short of available qualified drivers, Wheeler's position looked, er, safe, for the foreseeable future – unless something drastic happened. Happily, the day before last week's big freeze, it did.

Driving his new car, the prison's governor was approaching the bend at the bottom of the hill leading to the jail from one direction, while Wheeler, in the empty van, was accelerating towards it from the other. It was inevitable that one of the vehicles would end up in the ditch and, wouldn't you just know it, it was the governor's. His immediate call on his mobile to the activities manager (which apparently was heard two fields away) made it clear that there would be no second chances. Poor Wheeler was sacked.

But hang on a minute. Poor Wheeler? I think I know what my old pal Felix the Gambler would have said about the abrupt halting of the fast one's express taxi service, 'Poor Wheeler my arse!'

6 February 2003

The Poet's persecution

During our regular walks in the grounds here before reaching the paid-work stage, the Celtic Poet and I spent many happy hours putting the prison system to rights. But in our own cases we agreed that for all the setbacks, minor and major, we wouldn't have had it any other way. 'Even that thing with the mail?' I asked, the last time we spoke about the crazy days. 'Especially the thing with the mail,' he said.

It was a classic prison entanglement. The Poet moved from the Cat B where he and I had last been together to another Cat B further east. The PO (principal officer) who arranged the move was upbeat about it and told him, 'It's a progressive move. If you do well there, you'll get your Cat C in no time.' The Poet was pleased. A 'progressive move' for a lifer is a big event. Dormant feelings awaken. Hope is rekindled.

The euphoria lasts throughout the build-up to the move and rises during the move itself. It lingers through the reception process at the new jail, and for the first few days on the new wing it helps keep your tolerance level high, so that you don't flinch if your new cell is in rough order, full of graffiti, detritus or broken furniture. And you're unfazed by seemingly trivial infringements on your rights – up to a point. Like when the Poet went to collect his mail from the office a few days after landing at his new location.

A PO at the new prison handed him his letters and said, 'By the way, you've got a solicitor's letter there. I opened it by mistake, sorry.' Under prison rule 39, legal mail is privileged and should normally only be opened in the presence of the addressee. The Poet accepted the apology in good faith. Mistakes happen. So many letters arrive at a prison each day and all have to be opened and checked for 'illicit enclosures' before handing out. Easy to miss the solicitor's stamp. No reason to get paranoid.

When it happened again a couple of weeks later the Poet was irked. But again an apology was proffered. He was still a new face on the wing. Better to swallow – think about the Cat C. No good getting into conflict when you're still trying to make your mark. What a shame that so soon afterwards it had to happen a third time.

The Poet went to see the PO and explained. He acknowledged that with so much mail to check each day mistakes were bound to occur. But three times in a month? 'I'm just asking for rule 39 to be respected,' he concluded.

The PO had appeared to listen. He'd nodded in the right places and said 'Mmm' at appropriate moments. But the Poet knew exactly where he stood when the officer said finally, 'Troublemaker, eh?'

After breakfast a couple of days later the Poet's cell door was left locked at the call to labour. He got on his bell, but it went unanswered until movement to labour had ended. No apology this time, however. When his door was opened he got a ticking off. 'I suppose you want to go to work now?' said the officer, who had to summon a colleague to escort the Poet to the workshop.

Back at his cell that evening the Poet found that a 'nicking sheet' had been slid under his door. He'd been nicked (placed on report) for 'unauthorized absence from the workplace'. When he tried to explain to the wing officer that the landing officer had failed to open his door the answer was a curt, 'Explain it to the governor.'

The adjudication was brief. After the Poet finished stating his case the governor leaned back in his chair and said, 'Young man, if one of my officers tells me that he saw you riding around the wing on a motorbike, I want to know where you got the petrol from. Charge proved. Three days' CC.' (CC means cellular confinement – in the punishment block.)

Three days later the block officer opened the Poet's cell door. 'Right son. Back on the wing.' But the Poet had embraced the punishment of his persecutors. 'No,' he said. 'I'm staying down here.'

It was six months before the Poet decided his point had been made. When he did emerge his hair was a little longer, as was his beard. His skin was a little paler and he'd lost a little weight. But even though the whole episode cost him two years of 'progress' (delayed reports, postponed reviews), hats off to the man, his spirit was stronger than ever.

The parole board sits next month to consider the Poet's case for release. They'll have plenty of information on paper. But there will be so much about his experience that they can never know. I'm confident he's going to get a result, however. And I'm going to miss him when he goes.

13 February 2003

An encounter with crime

Three times I heard the well-spoken woman's voice in the background behind me before I realized what was going on. The first time her words had sounded so tentative they hardly registered. The train was packed with homebound travellers, most of whom I imagined, like me, were at the end of their working day. I had managed to get a seat at the back of the carriage near the centre door and it sounded like the woman was talking to someone in the space between the carriages.

The second time the woman asked her question she spoke louder and I noted the anxiety in her voice. 'Excuse me,' she said. 'Have you just taken something belonging to me?' There was no reason for me to take any notice. I thought she must have been speaking to a rail official – something to do with misplaced luggage, perhaps. Whatever it was, it was none of my business.

The third time she said it, however, there was no doubting her accusing tone and the increased anxiety in her voice. Down the quietened carriage faces were looking up and past where I sat. I, too, began to feel a little anxious. Suddenly the smartly dressed man in the seat opposite mine jumped up and strode past me towards the source of the voice. It occurred to me that he was the woman's husband. Along with everyone else now focusing in her direction, I heard the woman say, 'He's just had his hand in my bag and I think he may have taken something.'

'I do nothing,' said a heavily accented male voice. Seconds later the train moved off, only to judder to a halt after just a few yards. 'I do nothing,' the man protested.

Until the incident I had been sitting reflecting on my day in the office. My job for the charity is the first time in my life I have worked in a professional environment. It is mentally taxing – so much to do, never enough time to do it – but it can be rewarding at the same time. Gathering and collating information, writing letters, clarifying rules and regulations and just occasionally having a beneficial effect on someone else's life. Not something I had much experience of in my old life. During the past few months since starting paid work, I have had a taste of living the kind of life that I used to dream about in the closed-prison system. Having a responsible job, paying my way and being a regular citizen. When I'm out and about, going to and from work, nipping into cafés for a 'latte to go' or passing the time of day with a newspaper vendor, I seem to be blending in. Nobody gives me a second glance. And that's the way I like it.

But as the incident on the train appeared to be escalating I could feel my safe little world being shaken. There was the sound of a tussle and then a cry of 'He's gone!'

I began to relax, until the woman entered my carriage. The man who had vacated his seat and gone to her aid was behind her and motioned her to sit down opposite me. 'Thank you,' she said. The polite formality signified that they were, in fact, unknown to one another.

'I felt his hand in my bag,' the woman began to explain to those of us in the immediate vicinity. She was still shaken and grateful for the smart stranger's intervention. By the time the train driver entered the carriage the situation was stable. Someone pointed to the victim and the driver hurried over. 'Somebody came running down to the cab and alerted me,' he said. 'Thank you,' said the woman, 'but everything is fine now. I felt a hand in my bag...'

Nods and looks of exasperation were exchanged. I felt a twinge of guilt as she recounted what most us had already heard. Her ordeal had created an uncustomary sense of unity among the passengers. Somebody mentioned 'illegal asylum seekers'. Somebody else mentioned 'beggars'. The driver said, 'Things are getting worse.' All were in agreement about the common enemy, however: criminals.

In all the months since I've been going into the outside world this was the closest I had come to a crime. Along with everyone else, I had sympathized with the woman. My feelings of guilt and, I guess, responsibility, came from the long years of being part of a community that has been responsible for so much distress to others – a community constantly exposed to expressions of reproach and derogation from the rest of society. My status suddenly felt like a great dark secret. As the train pulled away again I wondered if anyone else in the carriage was guarding secrets.

20 February 2003

Heft's heavy load

The first time I saw Heft he must have weighed in at around nine and a half stone. Standing five foot five or five foot six at most, he wasn't exactly skinny, but he was lean and he had a mean look about him, though I believe this was an affectation designed to make up for his lack of physical stature. We were in the same 'local' jail then – both freshly sentenced and awaiting allocation to long-term high-security prisons.

Days in that jail were spent mostly in isolation – on single-cell bang-up – punctuated only by brief periods of unlock to collect meals, 'slop out' (empty toilet buckets), or walk for up to an hour in the caged exercise yard. But despite so little time spent out of the cells it was long enough to facilitate the exchange of important information. These momentary bursts of interaction were enough to learn how long other men were serving, who was in for what, who was not to be trusted. That was how I learned that Heft too was a 'lifer'.

Since we were on different landings we rarely came into contact with one another. But I witnessed him occasionally involved in arguments, in queues for meals, or for kit – usually trying to assert himself against the ignorance of those pushers-in who were unperturbed by the small man with the exaggerated glower. And when I was out in the yard I heard talk of him having the odd scrap in the slop-out recess following the arguments, none of which he ever walked away from victorious. There was no doubting that Heft was in for a rougher ride than many during his life sentence. But nobody sympathized, for everybody knew it was every man for himself.

I had been in the local jail a year when my allocation and transfer order finally came through. There were no long good-byes and very few short ones. Once in the back of the prison van heading north I gave little thought to those left behind. Then, five years and three transfers later, I bumped into Heft again.

It was during my first visit to the new prison's gym. A short man with shoulders as broad as the back end of a single-decker bus and legs like those of a shire horse was attempting a dead-lift of 250kg. The crowded gym had fallen silent in anticipation. The man kept his back rod-straight. He scowled and growled and suddenly roared 'Come on!' before bending his knees and grasping the bar aggressively with both hands. Then he began to pull. The strain on his body was unnatural. With muscles pumped to the maximum and teeth gritted, slowly he began to heave the bending bar off the floor and up on to his thighs. 'Good lift!'

called one of the PE instructors. The man held the bar for several seconds while his bulging eyes panned the room, before leaning forwards and letting the weights crash to the wooden platform, creating a cloud of chalk dust. 'Go on, Heft lad!' a voice cried out a fraction of a second before the eruption of a thunderous round of applause.

Heft stepped off the platform, rubbing his hands and grinning at his audience – unrecognizable as the man I remembered. Heft's 'rep' in that prison, I soon learned, was formidable. His weightlifting prowess commanded respect, admiration and fear in equal measure. Everyone acknowledged him when he passed by and nobody, but nobody, pushed in front of him in queues.

In later years in different jails I became aware that Heft's reputation had spread throughout the prison system. He had broken national prison power-lifting records, becoming one of a small group of prisoner strength athletes whose names are instantly recognizable to large numbers of prisoners across the country: a perfect example of successful adjustment to prison life, some might say.

When I landed in this resettlement prison I was not that surprised to find that Heft had landed here some months before me. He had done his time and addressed his 'offending behaviour' (by attending courses and programmes such as alcohol education, enhanced thinking skills and victim empathy). But neither was I surprised to learn that he was experiencing difficulties, particularly when he got a job as a factory hand just down the road from the prison. The other hands knew he was a prisoner and ensured that he was assigned the least popular tasks. He began absenting himself from the workplace in breach of his work-licence conditions. After a couple of warnings and a declined offer of counselling from the prison authorities he was 'grounded'. He grew less and less cooperative, until last week when he was returned to the closed system for 'failing to adjust to open conditions'. I have to say, I was not surprised about that either.

27 February 2003

Felix gets a golden letter

When Felix the Gambler told me and Big Rinty that he was no longer interested in being released, there was no doubt in our minds that he was serious. We had been talking about reviews and reports and the hoops we had to jump through to move through the system. It was evident that Felix had been suffering from hoop-jumping fatigue for some time.

The main problem was that different elements of the system had produced contradictory reports about our friend's situation. The recommendation after his last review, twenty months earlier, was that he should be transferred to an open prison. But before the transfer could take place he had received a visit from an outside probation officer. The visit lasted no more than fifteen minutes, but later the officer wrote a damning report based on the interview, using words and phrases which effectively branded Felix as an incurable criminal. This led to an intervention by the prison psychologist who ordered that Felix should partake in further offending-behaviour work 'just to be on the safe side'.

Felix's lawyer then commissioned a counter report from an independent psychologist, which led to the prolonged bout of wrangling between the lawyer, the experts and the prison authorities that had so far stymied Felix's progress. (In a lighter moment one evening, the Gambler identified an entertaining conundrum and declared insightfully to me and Big Rinty, 'If the experts are baffled, how can they be fackin' experts?') His disillusionment, however, was understandable. When Felix shared his thoughts on the matter with me and Rinty that night the big Dundonian and I shot each other a discreet look. But no response was necessary. Our friend wasn't fishing for our views or words of comfort or encouragement. He just needed to tell people he could trust of his intention, before he told the authorities. 'I've had long thoughts about this,' Felix added eventually. 'I can't... no, I refuse, to go along with their bollocks any more.'

It's one thing for a man serving a life sentence to decide in his mind that he never wants to be released (it can be a useful way of easing the psychological pressure that builds up during years of unbridled lusting for freedom). But it's rare that such thoughts get vocalized. Yet Felix went even further than that. He stated his position in a letter addressed to 'whom it may concern' and handed it to the PO responsible for lifers – the 'lifer PO' – to be forwarded to the appropriate administration official. But the PO did a good thing. He stuck the Gambler's letter in his drawer and said he would give it back when Felix changed his mind. He didn't know the notorious one as well as Big Rinty and I did.

Anyway, that was how things stood when I left my two pals more than a year ago for my own move to open conditions. At the time it felt like I was leaving a couple of fellow survivors behind in a disaster zone, my relief at getting away tempered by the uncertainty of their fate.

Rinty seemed to be in the stronger position of the two. He was only months away from an appearance in front of a panel headed by a judge to plead his case for release. His case was strong, but in the end not strong enough. He ended up with a two-year knock-back and a 'sideways move' – another closed prison and another offending-behaviour programme. By the time Rinty left Felix last autumn it had been almost three years since the Gambler's last review and still no date had been set for his next one. In his letters to me, Felix was adamant that he was expecting to be sent back to the high-security system at any time. But it made no difference. 'I'm not moving on this,' he reiterated.

To those who care about him, Felix's future looked bleak – until he received the golden letter from his lawyer explaining that a court had ruled that men serving discretionary life sentences, like Felix, were by law entitled to a review every two years. It meant in effect that Felix was being held unlawfully. The authorities were full of regret. They offered him an immediate transfer to an open jail and – wait for it – *compensation*. Six weeks later Felix got his move.

So can life inside get any more absurd? It seems so. Since being at the open prison Felix says he has 'not had a bet'. He says the acres of landscaped grounds are 'stunning' and that he spends most of his spare time walking and admiring the surrounding rolling countryside. 'I could never tire of this,' he wrote in his last letter. I've got to write to the Rint and tell him the good news. It looks as if Felix the Gambler has been transmogrified... into Felix the Rambler!

6 March 2003

The first Gulf War, I remember it well

It was Saturday teatime and I was standing minding my own business in the dining-hall meal queue. Around a quarter of the residents were out on town visits and would not be back until later, so the hall was quiet. As I looked around for a familiar face to eat alongside, the young man in front of me suddenly turned from his conversation with an associate and said to me, 'Do you remember the first Gulf War, mate?'

The first Gulf War? What was he on about? Obviously he was talking about the war between Iraq and the western allies in 1991. But I wasn't aware that there had been any more than one such war and said as much when I eventually answered.

The young man frowned. 'No, but there's gonna be,' he asserted.

Before I could say anything else the heavy-set man standing behind me interrupted, 'Yeah, there's gonna be another war,' he said, 'and as far as I'm concerned it's all wrong.'

The younger man disagreed. Jabbing a finger at the older man, he said, 'That Saddamfuckinhoosayne's out of order, mate. He needs sortin' out once and for all.'

Thankfully at that point the older man shook his head and decided against further discussion. The younger man looked to me again, but I'd managed to catch the eye of Tank, who was sitting in front of a giant plate of stew two rows from the serving counter. 'I'll be there in a minute,' I mouthed over the young man's head.

But he'd made me think of those first weeks of 1991. Lively weeks as I recall. How different my circumstances were then. Seven years into my sentence and still in the high-security prison system. They were strange days, looking back. My pal Sid used to call the way we lived 'a war of survival'. But you'd have to live for a while on a 'spur' in one of those places to really appreciate what he meant. A spur is a short, dead-ended corridor leading to a dozen or so single cells. In an establishment like the one that I was in at the time, there might be two or three spurs to a landing, two or three landings to a wing and up to six wings to the whole prison. The prisoners on my spur then were serving anything from ten up to thirty-five years. Since my arrival two years earlier there had been no other new faces.

To the untrained eye it would probably have looked like we all got along fine – and there were periods, short ones mind you, when we actually did: polite nods whenever we passed each other; friendly conversations; hooch- and drug-fuelled singalongs on a Friday night. Yet there was so much to that existence which could not be seen, could only be felt. And to feel it, you had to be a part of it. Only then would you know what it is to live down a trench in a psychological combat zone inhabited by your enemies. Only then could you understand how so much hatred can build up between men who are confined together year after year in such a way – a hatred that stays, for the main, in the mind, although it occasionally manifests itself in violence.

And the fear. Not necessarily the fear of attack, or of sustaining injury or even death from your enemies but, rather, the fear of losing control and ending up deeper in the trench – and for longer. The Bear couldn't handle it. He bowed out quietly after taking an overdose of smuggled-in sleeping tablets. Felch cracked too. He was an easy target with his skinny frame and prison-issue T-shirts that were always stained with his budgie's droppings. That's what Hacker the bodybuilder thought anyway, which was why he amused himself by subjecting the smaller man to months of torment and abuse – until the day Felch boiled up a pan of oil in the wing kitchenette and threw it across Hacker's back as he sat on the food-serving counter reading a newspaper. We never saw either man again.

And then there was Mr Abdellah. He was cooking a curry in the kitchenette at the same time as Little Legs was baking cakes. A birthday? A birth? Anything to celebrate and Little Legs would bake you a cake, for a small fee of course. That day there was an argument over whose turn it was to use the oven. Raised voices were raised higher. One man picked up the veg knife. It had only been signed out from the office tool-cupboard twenty minutes earlier. Seconds later the other man lay dying. No cakes that day – no curry either. My first Gulf War.

13 March 2003

Tank stands up for the workers

Tank is not a stupid man. But I thought he made a big mistake when he agreed to act as spokesman for disgruntled workmates at a nearby processing plant the other week. He had only had the position for a couple of months. I remember how pleased he'd been to get the job in the first place – how grateful. 'There were three of us going for the two vacancies,' he told me after his successful interview. 'I thought I'd have no chance being the only con.'

He had been interviewed by one of the men who owned the company. I imagine the man was impressed both by Tank's physical stature – most of his twenty-one-stone bulk is muscle – and by his gentle and reassuring manner. It's a package that never fails to throw people that don't know him. No doubt the boss thought differently, however, two months down the line.

When I asked the big man why he'd got so involved in the dispute his eyes widened. 'I was standing up for our rights,' he explained.

'Your rights?' I said. It seemed to me that Tank was being a little short-sighted. We had only known each other for eight or nine months when he first got the job. From our conversations, which usually took place as we worked out together in the gym or walked or jogged in the grounds in our free time, I found him to be a reflective, sensible man. But something here was definitely not making sense. 'Let me get this straight,' I said. 'You're in jail. A man gives you a job – over another who is not in jail and on the face of it is a good citizen, by the way – then once you've got your feet under the table you decide you've got rights?'

'Er, right,' said Tank.

'And now you've got no job?'

'Right.'

Tank stopped me mid-repetition during a gym workout once when he said out of the blue, 'I've really enjoyed my time in prison.' I almost dropped my dumb-bell on his foot. 'I've met some good lads,' he added, 'had a few laughs.' Well, I couldn't deny I'd had a few of those myself. But enjoyed my time in prison? That was the moment I concluded that Tank had not yet experienced enough deprivation, frustration, or vilification. In my view he was clearly a man in dire need of – dare I say it – more incarceration.

'I know it was unwise of me in the circumstances to stand up for the other workers,' he continued, as we analysed his situation post-paid employment. 'But there were principles involved.'

He explained that some of the machinery in the plant was obviously dangerous – guards missing, dodgy wiring etc. – and that workers were being forced to buy their own safety clothing with no subsidy. He said that the owners showed the workforce little respect and often spoke to individuals as if they were speaking to their serfs. It did shed a different light on the proceedings, I admitted. I said that was fair enough, but why not let somebody else take up the cudgels? As the only prisoner working there he was the most vulnerable. He had fewer rights than anyone else and he needed the money more than anyone else.

'That's where you're wrong,' he said. He told me that many of the other workers had been there a long time. 'Most of them are locals. It's not great money, but there's plenty of overtime and no travelling. They've got families, dependants. Believe me, I was probably the person there who least needed the money.'

There was little I could say to that. The fact that Tank's stance had had little if any effect on the company's working practices was irrelevant. It had cost him his job – the company later claimed that Tank had been on a three-month 'probationary period' and that he had not performed to a 'satisfactory standard'. And it may have had an impact on his chances of a successful parole application. But he was adamant that at the time it was the right thing to do and he did it. And, what is more, he would do it again, he said several times during our talk.

The more I thought about this afterwards the happier I was for Tank that he had just been in prison a couple of years. Without parole he's only looking at another year at most. He's still untainted. There are still few sides to his character. He still has but the one face. He was in prison, he recognized the right thing to do and regardless of the cost to himself he still had the courage to do it. Wonderful.

20 March 2003

Disturbing sounds

You learn early on in a prison sentence that behaviour by fellow prisoners which impacts on your well-being must be faced down at the earliest opportunity. Allowing irritations, intrusions, encroachments or infringements to continue unchecked for any significant length of time is a dangerous indulgence. You also learn, however, that responding appropriately is easier to think about than to do.

If you start off by communicating with your brother con too politely when violations occur – like this for example, 'Excuse me, do you mind not helping yourself to things in my cell that don't belong to you?' – you may well find yourself marked down as a soft touch, someone to be preyed upon. On the other hand, if you come across all aggressive, perhaps believing that attack is the best form of defence when you feel you've been slighted, in a meal queue for instance ('Oi! Twat! Who do you think you're pushing in front of?'), unless you have the physical attributes and psychological disposition to back it up, or unless you are connected to a well-known crime lord, you're likely to become embroiled in an unpleasant confrontation, possibly leading to a scalding, a chibbing (stabbing), or a whispering campaign ('He's a grass... he's a nonce...').

Two or three encounters like that are enough to undermine even the most assured character's ability to decide how to react. But it has to be sorted sooner or later. Otherwise you'll be destined for a hellish existence where your wants and needs count for nothing and every little inconvenience practised against you is amplified in your head. Acute paranoia may result – or worse, raving insanity. So pull yourself together, and act! Weigh up the situation. Check out the perpetrator discreetly. Plan your move with cunning and stealth.

I thought I'd left all that behind. I guess I've been shedding the shell I'd constructed around myself in the closed system ever since landing in open conditions over a year ago. It has been a pleasant softening process, this 'humanization'. But it can render you vulnerable. Like last week when my rest was interrupted several nights in a row.

Lying in the dark, listening to the thud, thud, thud of the bass line on the sound system belonging to my neighbour as it penetrated my ceiling and reverberated through the slats of my bed, I could feel the anxiety building in my stomach. It had gone 11pm, but instead of softening, the music seemed to be getting louder. I wondered if he'd fallen asleep with it on. I'd no idea who lived up there. It was a long trek around the corridors and up the stairs to reach his room to find out. And if he was sleeping through it, it would take more than a gentle tap on his door to rouse him. I drifted off, only to wake up again in the early hours to the same thud, thud, thud banging through my head. It was too late to go to his door. Wrong time of day to contemplate an argument...

Three nights of sleepless procrastination followed, before I snapped out of it. It was 10pm when he opened his door. I was greeted by a wall of sound. The man was young, early twenties, as I guessed he would be, but I was startled by his size as much as the noise. He stood no more than five and a half feet tall.

'Excuse me,' I began. I'd already committed myself to the polite approach but, seeing how small he was, I was suddenly emboldened. 'Do you mind turning that racket down?'

'What?' he said.

'The racket. Do you mind turning it down?'

Wide-eyed with indignation he glanced over his shoulder and then turned back to me and said, 'That ain't no racket, man. That's me sounds.'

'Sounds?' I spluttered. I was determined not to swear. 'Well, your sounds are keeping me awake,' I said. 'Do you mind keeping them down?' His sullen look told me he was unhappy at my request. 'Look,' I said. 'I've got to work all day. When I get back to the jail at night I've got to be able to sleep.'

'Work?' he said.

'Yes, work,' I said, still determined not to swear. Then I pointed. 'I work out there.'

'Oh, sorry,' he said, adding, 'I ain't been here long. I'll think on in future.'

'Thanks,' I said.

Satisfied, I returned to my room. As I went to sleep I thought about the chasm between my noisy neighbour and I. We were from different generations. We thought differently. And more than anything else, we had a different view of the world – inside and out.

27 March 2003

The war and dirty laundry

Since the new Gulf War started we've been having problems with the prison laundry man. His task is to provide service washes for those who are 'working out'. You drop your bag of washing off

in the morning and then collect it washed, dried and folded in a
neat little pile when you get in from work. That's the usual procedure, anyway.

Recently, however, people have been returning from work and
finding their dirty washing waiting for them, still dirty. It's not a
huge problem, just a mite inconvenient when you have to wait
until the weekend and do it yourself. But it seemed a shame as
he was good when he started – so conscientious and friendly –
always keen to make sure you got all your kit back. For some reason, he appeared to have turned grumpy and neglectful.

Last Sunday morning I managed to catch up with him and ask
him what had gone wrong. 'It's the war,' he said, baggy-eyed and
croaky-voiced. 'I'm up all night every night watching it on the
telly. I'm worried it's going to get out of hand.'

The prison had cable television installed a little while ago, and
one channel is piped through to the televisions in all the rooms.
The channel control is kept in the house office, and ever since
the new war in the Gulf started it's been set on a twenty-four-
hour news channel. Any time you like you can just flick it on and
catch up with all the action.

I imagine it's the same in prisons all over the country, since
most prisoners these days have televisions in their cells – unlike
the last time the country was at war in the Gulf. No televisions
in cells then – and no toilets, either, although the prison I was in
at the time had the most up-to-date toilet facilities. The system
was called 'night-san', short for night sanitation. The cell doors
were locked electronically, but if you needed the toilet you could
press a button on the cell wall, which would alert someone at the
control centre, who would unlock your door remotely. You then
had ten minutes to see to your needs. I remember the night-san
buttons were busy on the night the first Gulf War began. People
were taking longer, stopping to chat to pals and neighbours. 'It's
off' was the most frequently heard comment on the other side of
the door.

It was over an hour after I pressed my button before my door
was unlocked. Passing other cells as I walked down the spur, I

could hear all the radios tuned to the World Service. The shouting out of the windows had stopped early. People were thinking, no doubt wondering about what was to come.

At the time it was a common assumption among prisoners in the highest-security category (of whom there were several on my spur) that if ever there was a war, they would be summarily shot. But surely that only applied if it was a world war? Surely this little war in the Gulf wouldn't count? Nobody really knew.

Anxiety levels were high for the first couple of days. Everybody was talking about it. The television rooms were packed for the evening news bulletins. Instability on the other side of the wall made prison life feel more unstable. But things soon settled down. There was hardly a ripple in the daily routine. Breakfast was served at the same time, as were the rest of the meals. Cell doors were locked and unlocked at the same times. Exercise took place at the same time.

A sense of calm returned within a week. It was going to be a short war, most people agreed. It would have no real effect on our lives. We were soon back to focusing on the job in hand: getting on with doing our time, hoping for a quick peace, but not doing a very good job of living in peace with each other. For the six weeks or so that the war lasted, the only real difference on the wings and landings was that time spent on bang-up was quieter, as people spent more time listening to the news. I suspect it's much the same now, except, like our laundry man, they'll be watching it instead.

'You know,' said the laundry man as we chatted, 'I never appreciated how beautiful the world was until I came to prison. I took it all for granted – nature and that, friends and family. It's only since I've been inside that I've realized that it's the simple things in life that matter.'

I could only agree with him. He was entitled to worry and neglect his washing duties if he wanted to. After all, I concluded, on the scale of the world's problems, what's a bag of washing?

3 April 2003

27

No news from the Guru

A letter received by a man in a neighbouring room this week brought news of a former associate. Sadly it was only by chance that the news reached me at all. My neighbour was talking to another neighbour as I passed by in the corridor. 'They used to call him the Guru...' I heard him say. There was only one 'Guru' that I knew of and that was Stu, who, along with Big Rinty, I had got to know in my first long-term prison, fourteen or fifteen years ago.

The last time I saw Stu was just over two years ago – on the morning of his transfer to an open prison. It was a January morning, clear blue and frosty, and Big Rinty and I helped him carry his stuff (books mostly) over to reception.

Stu was obviously keen to get away, nobody could blame him for that. But it was an odd parting. As we sat together in the big holding room waiting for the Group 4 wagon to arrive, I thought I detected a hint of embarrassment in Stu's manner. The small talk was hard going. It was a joyous occasion certainly, since it had taken our pal nineteen years to get the move. Yet there was also a sense of awkwardness, the cause of which I couldn't quite put my finger on. Stu's curtness with Rinty was out of character too. The big Dundonian went back further than I did with Stu. They had been located in adjacent cells for some years before I arrived at the jail where I first met them.

Rinty was talking about their old days – before I came on the scene. Stu didn't seem too keen on being reminded. Eventually he stopped him. 'That's the past,' he said, 'we've go to look forward now, man.' Well, that was easy enough for him to say, since at the time his forward was looking a sight more certain than either of ours – and Rinty's especially was the least certain of all of us. I squirmed for him, deciding not to try to raise a smile by remembering the times many years earlier when we used to huddle around Rinty's radio in the exercise yard on a Sunday morning listening to the Classic Gold station, waiting to see if any of our dodgy requests would get mentioned. I was going to recall the one that we did 'for Spanner from Andrella,' who, the DJ told the whole world, 'wants him to know that no matter what anyone says she'll always be waiting for him.' Andrella – born Andrew – was the make-up-wearing prison library orderly whose campaign for a sex-change and a transfer to a women's jail was the cause of many a heated debate on the wings and landings.

Our prank was juvenile, I know, but how it made us howl when the request was broadcast – and then again and again whenever we spotted Spanner getting chased out of the library by an irate, handbag-swinging Andrella. Stu's snap at Rinty, however, told me that it was the wrong time to recall this silly jape.

We'd all grown up a bit since then I suppose. Rinty was still game for an inappropriate laugh of course, and I guess I was too occasionally. But Stu had had a serious head on his shoulders for a while – ever since he'd got religion. Though to be fair, nobody doubted the sincerity of his devotion to the Christian faith, which inspired him to learn to play the guitar and write and perform gospel songs in the prison chapel. Eyebrows were raised when he began studying psychology, mind you. But he took that seriously too, gaining a degree in the subject and then his master's. Such interests could have left him isolated on the landings. Instead he found that he'd created a new role for himself. People were aware that he was not playing at religion or education. He was not a 'dabbler', trying to impress or 'graft' for 'brownie points'. As he grew spiritually and intellectually it appeared that he began to emanate a quiet sagacity, which fellow prisoners found attractive. And he was happy to listen to troubles, offer advice or even mediate in quarrels. He built a solid reputation and gained an apt and wonderful nickname: the Guru.

Stu said he would write and let us know how he was once he'd settled down. We waited and waited, but no letter arrived. Now and again we had word, usually from somebody sent back to the closed system. According to other sources he was always 'doing fine' or 'doing well'. It would have been nice though to have heard from him personally. The news according to my neighbour's neighbour's friend is that after twenty-one years in prison the Guru has been released. I'll write tonight and let Rinty know.

10 April 2003

A surprise for a beggar

It was the end of the first really warm day of the year. My head was still full of my day's work: enquiries received, information retrieved, letters written. I had never considered before that 'office work' could be so demanding – or so satisfying. Not for the first time as I made my way to the station through the crowded and anonymous streets did I take a deep breath and wonder at my good fortune. Then I heard the man's voice. It was so close it had to be directed at me. 'Excuse me, can I interest you in some life insurance?' I smiled inwardly, pleased that I'd been mistaken for a regular citizen.

'I'm sorry...' I began, turning to politely dismiss my accoster, before confusion stopped me saying anything else. His appearance was not what I expected. He was tall and young, no more than nineteen or twenty years old. Despite deep pockmarks, the pink skin on his face had a fresh glow about it, though sleep residue remained clogged in the corners of his smiling, bright-green eyes. Most telling were his ill-fitting clothes and his recently hacked red hair which sprang from his head like the contents of a burst cushion. He was obviously homeless and begging and the life insurance quip was his in-line. I hadn't heard that one before.

'No thanks pal,' I said, acknowledging his sense of fun. By now he was striding alongside me, grubby paper cup held hopefully in front of him. 'My life wouldn't be worth your trouble,' I added.

Pleased that I had engaged with him, he stepped up his pace and his grin broadened. 'What about double glazing then?'

I thought that was funny and I laughed. But then I felt uneasy.

Such encounters have become regular occurrences. Too regular. Responding to people who survive in this way is getting harder. Only the other week I talked about it to the Celtic Poet. Like me, he had lived on the streets on and off for a number of years before his life sentence. He is philosophical about those times now, but he hasn't forgotten.

'I never pass by a *Big Issue* seller without buying a copy,' he told me. He said he often takes the time to stop and chat with vendors and he's happy to reveal his own experiences. 'I don't lecture anybody,' he said, as we strolled around the football field, 'but if I pick up that they're prepared to listen, then I try and introduce the idea that whatever happens to us, we can still lift ourselves. We mustn't ever give up.' He turned and prodded his chest before adding, 'Don't forget, I was on the streets long before the *Big Issue*.' That was another thing the Poet and I had in common – and the main reason for my discomfort in these situations.

For how could it be that my life should have been so chaotic and meaningless all those years ago? Yet here I am now after almost nineteen years in prison, with a job, a direction and a purpose. I told the Poet that I rarely gave money to people on the streets. 'Why not?' he asked. 'Because it's never going to be enough,' I said.

Back near the station the red-headed young man persisted. 'So no double glazing?' he said. 'Well, how about...' At that moment I decided to talk to him – and, however unwisely, to reveal my circumstances. 'Hang on a minute,' I said, stopping on the pavement and turning to face him. On either side of us people streamed by. I pulled a handful of change from my coat pocket and dropped it into his cup.

That should have been the end of our encounter. But before he could walk away I said, 'Actually, I do have double glazing already – in my prison cell.' This revelation appeared to have no effect on him.

I went further and told him how long I'd been in jail and that the reason that I was out and about and able to stand talking to him was because I was being prepared for release. He stopped smiling and dropped his eyes. He thought I was kidding him on. 'Look,' I said and produced my prison ID card. 'That's me: Convict 99.' His green eyes widened. 'I don't know what's happened in your life,' I went on, 'but what I'm trying to say is that broken people – people like us – we can be fixed.' Of course, I hadn't taken into account the possibility that he might not want fixing. He had a right to give me some abuse if he wanted and I waited for it. Instead he suddenly thrust out his free hand and beamed at me. 'Fucking hell, man!' he said.

I shook his hand and mirrored his face-wide smile – and on that salubrious note, we parted.

17 April 2003

Freedom, he wrote [This article announced the publication of *A Life Inside*, April 2003]

It was the prison chaplain's wife who first gave me an inkling that I might have a talent for writing. Her name was Grace and she had volunteered to run an evening class in the prison's education department on the perils of drinking too much alcohol. Her class took place just one evening a week, but it got us off the wing for an hour and a half. More importantly, Grace was an attractive, open-hearted woman who treated everyone as equal. The content of the course didn't matter too much. An hour and a half in her company was enough to make a prisoner feel like a human being again – for a while, anyway.

Grace used to give us 'homework' to do in our cells. (Is alcohol a stimulant or a depressant? What are the damaging effects of over-indulgence? How many units of alcohol can a man safely drink per week? How many for a woman?) After the fourth or fifth session, she pulled me to one side at the end of class. She thanked me for the effort that I had made with my homework – and then she said, 'Can I ask you, do you write?'

An odd question, it seemed. 'Well, yes...' I said.

She smiled, acknowledging my puzzlement and then said: 'No,

do you write? Are you a writer?'

This time it was my turn to smile. 'Oh no,' I said, 'no, not at all.'

A writer? If anyone else had asked me such a question, I would have thought that they were winding me up. But Grace had been sincere. She hardly knew me. It was my first long-term prison and I had only been in the place a few months. With just a few hundred words of my untidy handwriting in her hands, Grace had really thought that I might be a writer. It was the first time since my life sentence began that anyone had suggested that I might possess a positive quality. Somehow being alone in my cell that night didn't feel so bad.

Grace had awakened a memory from my childhood. My young life had been unstable and it was not until the age of eleven that I started to attend school regularly. That was when I was sent to live in a council-run home. I was a surly, incommunicative student in most subjects at school. But I shone at English, something for which it appeared that I had a natural aptitude, sharing the top spot in the class with a boy called Michael, who I now understand suffered from a form of autism. It was always a race between Michael and I to get our hands up first in spelling lessons. Whenever I took my report card back to the home at the end of term, however, nobody thought to acknowledge that I might have achieved something with my A grades in English composition and comprehension. There was no abuse that I knew of in the home. But neither was there any encouragement or sense that any of us in there would amount to very much. In the end I left school when I left the home, aged fifteen, with no academic or vocational qualifications. From then on I only ever had a very poor view of my intellectual abilities. Grace's comments took me back to those school days when I secretly believed I was good at something. She had made me think that perhaps it was something I was still good at.

Eventually I began getting call-ups to see the wing psychologist, Joan, who was approaching the end of her career. Over a period of several months, Joan persuaded me to attend academic education classes. She lent me books by Solzhenitsyn and Dostoevsky. 'You're bright,' she would say. 'You must educate yourself.' Flaubert and de Maupassant followed, and within a year I had an English O level, grade A. When Joan retired, she gave me a copy of Solzhenitsyn's *Cancer Ward*, along with a card in which she had written, 'Today is the first day of the rest of your life.'

These early encounters fashioned the path that the rest of my life in prison would take. Education would be the mainstay. I was accepted on an Open University course, choosing to do an arts degree, majoring in history. My studies, for the most part undertaken in my cell at night, took me from classical Greece through Rome's Augustan Age; covered culture and beliefs in Europe during the Middle Ages, the Age of Enlightenment, and Victorian Britain; and concluded with a comparative study of the effects of industrialization in Great Britain and the US from the mid-nineteenth century to the present day. Along the way I gained a reputation in the various prisons in which I was located for being able to 'write a good letter'. Fellow prisoners would ask, usually through mutual associates, if I could assist with parole representations, letters to probation officers or social services, or just wing applications to the governor.

Life on the concrete and steel of the landings could be bleak and merciless, but over the years I met a number of well-disposed people who worked in the prison service, as well as many remarkable fellow prisoners – all of whom assisted in making it possible to turn a life around. Most importantly, perhaps, I discovered that education, and writing in particular, freed my mind so that being bound became my means of liberation – liberation from a past that was more constricting than any prison sentence ever could be.

It took me ten years to establish a way of living that I believed was authentic. After that it was just a question of doing the time. I got involved in prisoner representation groups, charity fundraising events and prison magazine projects while working as a hospital orderly, gym orderly, workshop hand and yard cleaner. More years passed and then came the opportunity to write for the *Guardian*. By then I was in a medium-security prison, where I thought it would be easier to take advantage of such an opportunity, although my first attempt to contact the paper almost ended in disaster.

In large black type at the back of the phonebooth, the sign was in plain view for all to see: ANY PRISONER FOUND CONTACTING THE MEDIA WILL BE PLACED ON REPORT. Nobody using the phone could miss it. Except that I had – and I knew that once the security staff had listened to the tape recording of my conversation, I would be in trouble. The phone I had used was on the hospital wing. Unlike the phones on the main wings, it was left switched on all day and there was never a queue, so I had managed to persuade a healthcare officer to let me in on the pretext of arranging a dentist's appointment.

Once in my cell I thought about the possible consequences of my call. A few days earlier I had received a letter from a writer friend who told me that someone he knew at the *Guardian* had mentioned that the paper was thinking about running regular articles from a serving prisoner. My writer friend said that he had put my name forward as a possible candidate and then an editor had asked if I could call him at the paper to discuss it. Now it looked like I had stymied my chances before writing a single word. Once my 'contact with the media' had been discovered, I would be nicked and put in the punishment block for sure. In itself this would be no real hardship – but it would make any further communication with the newspaper difficult, if not impossible.

Then I had an idea. When the cell doors were unlocked again, I went to the wing office and asked if someone would ring through to the hospital for me. I described the officer that I had spoken to earlier and said that I wanted to see him again. 'I need to talk to him about an urgent personal matter,' I said. The young wing officer must have thought that I had an unmentionable medical condition as he gave me a look which said 'say no more' and promptly made the call.

I had prepared a little file containing evidence of my writing activities to take with me. It included a couple of letters that I had had published in local newspapers, a certificate for winning first prize in the prose category of the Koestler Awards (an annual arts competition for prisoners and patients in 'special' hospitals), and one or two bits from prison magazines.

Back in the hospital I sat in the office on the other side of the decent officer's desk. 'Right,' he said. 'What's this urgent problem?'

I took my file from under my arm and began spreading bits of paper on his desk. 'If you'll just bear with me a moment,' I said, 'I'd like to explain something about the way I've been serving my time.'

He looked slightly bemused but allowed me to continue. I told him that I had been in prison for fifteen years. 'I've tried to use the time constructively,' I said. I explained about the evening education classes and the degree. Pointing to my bits of paper, I spoke about my writing ambitions. 'Prison has given me opportunities to develop in a way that would never have happened outside,' I said. 'It has enabled me to become the person I think I could have been if things in my early life had been different.'

'I don't mean to be rude,' he said, 'this is great stuff. All credit to you. But what has it got to do with me?'

'Well,' I said, 'when I used the hospital telephone this morning, I called an editor at the *Guardian* newspaper.' I explained everything and how I had missed the sign forbidding prisoners from contacting the press until I had put the phone down. 'As soon as security hear the tape I'll be nicked and in the block.'

'Hmm,' he said, looking thoughtful. He looked up. He reached across to the tape machine which held the cardphone's security tape and pressed the eject key – then he lifted the tape out and slid it into the top pocket of his starched white tunic.

'When they come to collect it tonight,' he said, 'I'll just have to tell them I forgot to put a tape in this morning.'

I managed a choked 'Thanks' as I gathered up my papers.

The editor that I had spoken to asked me to write some articles about prison life. 'Give me two or three, at about eight hundred words,' he said. Late nights followed. I scribbled like a madman. In the mornings my cell floor was littered with balls of screwed-up sheets of A4 paper. But finally I had three pieces (words counted meticulously). I posted them off first class and then waited. Eventually, a reply arrived.

'Thank you for your pieces,' the editor wrote. 'We can certainly use them in some form or other.' At first, officials in the prison were far from encouraging. 'If I was you I'd pick another pastime,' said one senior teacher in the prison's education department when I approached her with my letter from the *Guardian*. An assistant governor was even more direct. 'Well,' he began, 'I could give you one big no, or fifty small no's – but the answer would still be the same I'm afraid.'

Happily, though, prison-service headquarters were more positive. When the *Guardian* explained what my contributions to the paper would entail and gave an assurance that prison rules governing prisoners' contact with newspapers would be rigorously adhered to, an official agreed to put the proposal to the prisons' minister. A few weeks later we got the good news: the minister was 'content for this to go ahead'.

It had taken a year to get official approval. It meant that I could telephone the paper whenever I needed to, so long as I had a phonecard. All seemed fine – except that now, of course, I had to start writing for real. It was a scary moment. If I had known then the internal agonies and pressures I would experience while endeavouring to meet deadlines – phoning copy through in the midst of crises and dramas, sweating blood sometimes as I laboured over a final sentence – well, the truth is I would still have gone for it.

21 April 2003

Mystery new man on the block

How time flies. It's hard to believe that I've been in open conditions for a year and a half already. Not a long time when you're in the closed system, sure enough, but significant here. You only have to look at the turnover. Every other week there is movement out and movement in. So many old faces gone, so many new ones arrived. I'm definitely in the category of 'old hand' in this place now – status that takes years to achieve in a closed jail.

Since I've been working full time, it's rare that I'm even 'in' during the week. This means that meeting new arrivals has to wait until the weekends, although weeks pass sometimes before such acquaintances are made. New men always stand out at first. They are either overly talkative with relief at being away at last from the oppression of the wings – or they are cautious and hesitate to engage. The latter reaction is more common in men who have spent a long time behind high walls. The new man I met in the library on Sunday morning fitted into neither category, however.

I was browsing through the newspapers when he appeared alongside me and spoke. 'It's changed a bit since my last stint here.' It was not an untypical opening line for a prison conversation, but unusual here since resettlement prisons have the lowest re-offending rates of any type of prison. Not only that, but people who fail after a chance at a place like this don't normally get another – at least not at the same one.

When I turned I found myself looking into two brown eyes that shone like polished chestnuts. The slim-built man wasn't smiling, but his narrow, lived-in face appeared friendly enough. His neatly trimmed hair and matching beard were flecked with grey and at a guess I would have said he was in his mid- to late-fifties.

'Is that so?' I said, turning back to the papers. 'When was that then?'

'1963,' he replied.

If I'd been drinking a cup of tea I'd have spluttered into it. 'You're kidding.'

'I'm not,' he said. 'It was a detention centre then. I was fifteen and got three months. This is the first time I've been in trouble since.'

Forty years on. It was hard to get my head around such a period of time. Not the time itself but the fact that it was outside time. I met a man once who had spent forty straight years in prison and was still a Cat A – the highest security category in the system. That forty-year stretch was a long time, especially in comparison to the puny seven years I had served up until then. But forty years in prison does not tally with forty years in the outside world, for prison time – time spent deprived of intimacy, emotional fulfilment, social intercourse, friendship, family and love – is pure time, measured not by births, marriages and deaths, but by annual reviews and knock-backs.

The new man told me his name was Jed and that he was in the last twelve months of a 'three' (a three-year sentence). We retired to the easy chairs at the back of the library to chat. I was eager to know how it felt to return to the same prison after a forty-year interlude and he was keen to tell me. 'It's creepy,' he said when I asked him outright. 'Walking over paths that I had to quick-march over then. All the shouting and bawling – the screws that was – we weren't allowed to talk, not at all, except for half an hour after tea.'

He went into detail about his formative experience. His three months were served in the winter. He talked about the boys having to parade in the courtyard in short navy jackets and grey flannel trousers at six o' clock in the morning. As he spoke, other library users gathered around the two of us. Occasionally he paused, staring momentarily – not into space, but into time. His descriptive narrative made it easy to imagine the flickering scenes he was recalling.

He mentioned the prison officers. 'There was Mobile – so called because of his habit of shouting "Get mobile, lad!" whenever he caught anybody idling – and Biffo with the big ears; "you people!" he used to call us...'

Jed kept us engrossed with his tale for so long that we were almost late for lunch. He continued as we made our way to the dining hall. 'I'm telling you, it was forty years ago...' he must have told a dozen people.

How time flies, I remember thinking.

24 April 2003

ERWIN JAMES

Tank's principles

It wasn't the end of the world for Tank when he lost his job at the processing plant the other month. There were no worries about how he was going to pay the rent. He still had a bed at night and food on his plate. And best of all, he had managed to save a few hundred pounds from the wages he had been picking up for the two and a half months he had held the position. But it was still a major setback for the big man.

I'm thinking about his parole prospects, I suppose. For all his exhortations about not having had such a bad time in prison, like any rational person he would rather be out than in – and sooner, rather than later. Another year in prison is at stake. My guess, however, is that the parole board will consider his sacking as a failure to demonstrate a commitment to resettlement and therefore be minded to decide against him.

But let's just review the situation for a moment. In its brief memo to the relevant governor, the company said it had had to 'let him go' because he hadn't 'performed to a satisfactory standard' during his three-month probationary period. No mention was made of the fact that, on behalf of his fellow workers, he had confronted bosses at the plant with safety concerns and complaints about dubious working practices two days before he collected his P45.

Nobody can blame the company, of course. It did give him a chance and he turned out to be a thorn in its side. Once he had left their employ, whatever happened to him was not its concern. But doesn't Tank deserve some credit for taking a principled stance against a situation he believed needed some redress?

At first, when I found out what he had done and the price he had paid, my view was that Tank had been foolish. It was only after thinking about it and having some discussions with my big pal that I conceded that he had done a good thing – a great thing, in fact. It is so easy to be seduced by the path of least resistance during a prison sentence. Time in jail constantly forces the

40

prisoner to seek out and even engineer circumstances that are most favourable to personal well-being. Integrity exists, but only on a very long sliding scale. A veteran of long-term imprisonment told me years ago, 'If you want to stay sane in these places, always be prepared to compromise.' But too much compromise can make a character flabby and ineffective. Sometimes a man needs to make a stand just to feel alive.

In the house-block, opinion was divided. And understandably so. It's hard enough to get a job on the out, never mind while still doing time. Everybody in the prison is acutely aware of that hard fact. Which was why some were angry with Tank for apparently throwing away a perfectly good source of income. They were scathing and made comments about him not being 'up to it'.

'That workers' rights business was a load of bollocks. It was an excuse,' they said. 'He just couldn't hack hard graft,' was the truth according to that camp. (Though nothing was said to Tank's big face.)

Nobody who associated with him doubted his motives, however. On the out he had been a dry-stone waller. He had photos on the picture board in his room of some of the magnificent walls he had built in the past. Whatever anybody says, hard graft does not come much harder than that. In any case, at the end of the day, the opinions of fellow cons are irrelevant. It's the parole board that will decide the merit of Tank's case and any day now it will be considering.

The good news is that, in the meantime, Tank has not been idle. With the help of Mrs B, the vocational-training coordinator, he managed to enrol on an HGV driving course. The money he had saved was all he had in the world, but he pledged it to Mrs B for the course and she got him the rest from her 'special fund'. His test was on his birthday. That night he knocked on my door and told me, 'The examiner said, "I'm sorry to tell you you've failed. Nevertheless, many happy returns for the rest of the day."'

Poor Tank. We spent a few minutes calling the examiner nasty names and then I said, 'Hombre, it's time to dig in.' And he did. He put his name down for the first available test date and when he took it again he passed. It gets better. Last Monday he started work for a local haulier. So you see, my big friend is committed to a successful resettlement – as well as being principled. Let's just hope that the former is enough to get him a result from the parole board.

1 May 2003

The green-eyed stranger

Larrson looked familiar the first time I saw him. It was teatime, and he was sitting in the corner of the dining hall with a group of other young men, all in their early to mid-twenties. With his pale skin, large, shaved head and piercing green eyes he would have stood out in any crowd. But there was something else about him – something I couldn't quite put my finger on – that gave me the feeling that he and I had met somewhere before.

He was obviously well known to the people with whom he was sitting. Their table was the noisiest in the hall and nobody got into their company unless they were also considered to be 'one of the chaps' (latest trainers, designer tops). But unless he was really ten years older than he looked, he was too young to feature in my prison history. So where did I know him from?

That teatime was Larrson's first day in the jail. I'd been here about six months and had just started going out of the gate on unescorted community work, so it was a while before he and I found ourselves in a position to have a conversation – months after he'd landed in fact. By then he was working as the prison gym orderly. It was the end of a Saturday morning session when we spoke, and he was going around tidying up the weights. He nodded when he got to my spot and said, 'Finished?'

I told him I had, and offered to give him a hand to put the rest of the equipment away. 'How's it going?' I asked.

'All right thanks,' he said.

I'd noticed that he was no longer one of the regulars on the noisy table in the dining hall. He still sat there occasionally, but clearly had not aligned himself with 'the chaps' on a full-time basis. Well done to him, I remember thinking. It can be extra difficult being your own man in prison once you have been welcomed into a clique. Peer pressure can be particularly intense inside, especially among younger prisoners. But Larrson seemed to be managing well enough at doing his own thing and still keeping the respect of his pals.

We talked as we racked the dumb-bells. He'd settled in well, he told me. He was thrilled with his gym job and had eighteen months left to serve. I told him about my community work, and said that if he kept going the way he was, he too would be out of the gate on his own before he knew it. His green eyes lit up at that. 'Can't wait,' he said.

I found him a pleasant and easy man to speak to, but I was disappointed not to feel a stronger sense of recognition once we had actually engaged. I'd been so sure that I knew him from somewhere. But it wasn't until we'd finished putting the kit away and were making our way back to the house-block that I broached the subject. 'I know it's unlikely,' I said, 'but I've got this odd feeling that I've seen you before.'

'I don't think so,' he said. He told me he was twenty-two, and that this was his fourth prison sentence since the age of sixteen. He was now doing a 'five' (five-year sentence), which he'd started off in a young offenders' institution. The closed prison he'd been in before getting his D Cat was his first experience of the adult system.

'It wasn't as bad as I'd been told to expect,' he said, 'but fuck going back there after this.' I concurred with him on that point, and just as we were about to part on the house-block steps he added, 'It all went wrong for me after I was on the documentary.'

'Documentary?' I said.

'Yeah. I was on probation. These people came from the television. There was a few of us – all sixteen. They followed us for weeks. It was a buzz at first, but after it was on the telly it turned into a nightmare.'

He said he'd 'played up' in front of the cameras. 'I was only on probo for allowing myself to be driven in a nicked motor. Next thing I know, I'm our estate's version of Attila the Hun.'

Had I seen the programme? I couldn't be sure. Six years had passed since it had been aired. But it did ring a very loud bell. We did a lap of the football field and he told me more. Following the screening, his family had received hate-mail and he'd been shunned by employers. 'After that, it was all downhill,' he said.

The chat I'm talking about took place last summer, and I still can't say if I saw that programme. But the other week Larrson started working out on paid employment and we managed to have another talk at the weekend. He sounded on good form. He's working on a building site. He says it's the first proper job he's ever had.

8 May 2003

The big bang

Even after a year and a half of being here, the view over the valley from the lower compound of this relatively open prison still evokes powerful feelings. I'll never forget the first time I stood at the top of the slope and looked beyond the fence at the acres of fields and woodlands. I think it gave me a sense of how it must feel for a climber to stand on the summit of a mountain he thought unconquerable. All those years, head down and focused, determined to achieve something from this experience, but so often uncertain about what it was exactly that I was trying to achieve.

And the times when I thought I would be defeated. Those were the hardest. Not hard physically, or psychologically even, but something even deeper. Because if I failed in creating something positive from the whole situation, then what would have been the point?

After arriving at my first long-term prison, I was called to the governor's office. He asked me what my sentence was, and, even though he had my file in front of him and obviously knew perfectly well the answer to his question, I told him. 'And how are you feeling about it?' he said. I told him I was fine about it. It had come as no surprise. I was adjusting well, I thought. He kept his eyes locked on mine and asked, 'Have you thought about how you are going to manage the years ahead?'

To tell the truth, I hadn't. For the first year after my trial I'd been kept in the virtual solitary confinement of twenty-three-hour bang-up. I'd got it into my head that it was possible to change, but it was only an idea. The change that was necessary in my case was so big. How does anyone change a whole life? The isolation of the year's bang-up had helped to clear my head and allowed me to organize my thoughts in a way that would never have been possible in my life before prison. But I was still a long way from figuring out what my goal was. I told the governor that I wasn't sure how I was going to manage it – but manage it I would. 'That's good to hear,' said the governor, 'but it's going to hit you eventually. Just be ready for it when it does.'

Later, I learned that prisoners serving the longest sentences are normally moved around the prison system every few years. The 'optimum' time for a man to spend in a dispersal (highest-security) prison, for example, is three to five years. Yet on that first long-term wing I met men who had been in that same prison for ten, twelve, and in one case fifteen straight years. It was a relief, on the one hand, to be away from the bang-up. But relief was tempered by the thought that I might end up like some of those wasted people. How could I avoid that?

'Use the time, don't let the time use you,' was one of the gems of advice from a pal I made on the wing. Dave, a former post-man, was years ahead of me in his life sentence and he seemed to have a grip on it. I drank in his wisdom, but so much of how a man adjusts to endless years in prison seemed to depend on luck. Not only did you need to have the right attitude, but you need-ed a strong character and a forceful personality. And, if the evidence from my life before prison was anything to go by, I had none of the required qualities. Somehow they had to be developed.

I remember telling Dave once, some months after I had enrolled in education classes, that I had coined my own motivational phrase. 'Listen,' I said, 'I'm going to make this a scholastic monastic experience.' Dave chuckled and said, 'Now you're getting it, mate.'

As I got into a routine of churning out the weeks and months – in the education department, with my books, in the gym, running around the football pitch – I became aware that subtle personal developments were taking place. Subconsciously I was stripping myself down and then gradually rebuilding, and never once during that time did I think of the governor's warning – until it hit me. A black, lethargy-inducing cloud. Just to get out of bed in the morning was a struggle. 'Come on!' I used to command myself as I threw back the covers. 'Feel good! Feel strong!'

I'm still not sure how I got through it. But I think about those dark months every time I go down to the lower compound. The sky over the valley always looks so big. Sometimes I wish I could stand and gaze into the distance forever.

15 May 2003

Mally finds love a pain

Mally began showing signs of distress months ago. The increased volume of his requests to fellow prisoners for 'roll-ups' and 'tea bags' was the most obvious. But more significant was his insistence on discussing the merits of his forthcoming parole review over and over again with whomever he struck up conversation. 'So what do you think?' he would ask. Except that he didn't really want to know what you thought if it wasn't what he wanted to hear.

In spite of his odd demeanour, most people thought he would walk when the parole board finally considered his case. The only caveat was that he should be cautious in his anticipation. But Mally would entertain no opinions that included any urging to be cautious. 'They've got to let me out,' he would insist, sometimes aggressively. 'I've done twice as long as I was supposed to. I can't do any more.'

Along with several others, Mally had been a regular visitor to Tam the Man's room before Tam's release, but I was never really sure about his relationship with the barrel-shaped Scotsman. Like Tam, Mally had had a taste of freedom many years earlier. He'd served eleven years of his life sentence before he was first transferred to an open prison, only to abscond at the first opportunity. After a few days of living rough he was recaptured and returned to the closed system, where he remained until eight or nine months ago when he got a move to this place. By then he'd been inside for twenty-two years.

There was always a good atmosphere when people congregated in Tam's room – funny stories being told, banter and gentle ribbing being exchanged. But I noticed that there was underlying antagonism between Mally and Tam. Tam would often refer to Mally as 'the Numpty' – and not just behind his back. It didn't help that Mally took a job as a 'Womble' (a prisoner who wanders the grounds with a bin bag in one hand and a litter picker in the other). Or that the way he spoke to people often got him into unnecessary arguments, especially with those doing relatively short sentences, who were more likely to react negatively to his anxious pleading. Over time he lost his credibility, and I think Tam was unforgiving because he himself had been through the mill and managed to come out the other end through sheer determination. It left him with no sympathy for anyone who was not prepared to make at least the same effort.

Mally appeared to take the ridiculing well. But I felt that he was tolerating it just so he could stay in the company. His distress probably made him believe that it was better to have pals and be the butt of jokes than to be isolated. But the company came to an end when Tam was released at the beginning of the year and Mally was left with no regular associates.

Soon afterwards, Mally began going out on hostel leave in preparation for life outside. The monthly leaves went well enough as far as I was aware, though whenever he got back there was nobody for him to talk to about his experiences. He spoke to me occasionally, and now and again to the Celtic Poet. Sometimes he spoke to Tank. But none of us really had the time that he needed. You get in from work, you read for an hour or so or watch a bit of television, and then it's time for bed. Once you're working out, you hardly see people in the jail. It's not unusual, for example, for a couple of weeks to pass between the Poet and I having a talk, and we only live three doors apart. Weekends are the only time that there is any free time, but unless arrangements are made, who knows who is going to be around for a friendly chat?

This was the situation Mally found himself in, I think. So much happening in his life, but nobody on the wing to share it with. The last time I spoke to him he told me he'd met a woman. 'She's lovely,' he said. A couple of weeks later I learnt from the Poet that the woman hadn't known Mally was in jail. Mally was beginning to feel so strongly about her that he decided to tell her and chose to do so over the telephone. 'She hung up on him,' said the Poet. 'He's gutted.'

The next thing I heard was that Mally had returned early from a leave one morning last week covered in bruises. The following day he was shipped back to a closed prison. His parole review will still take place next month. But there's no chance now of the result he was hoping for. Goodness knows how he's coping.

22 May 2003

Tank gets parole but it's not all good news

The knock on my door was loud and rapid. It was almost teatime and I could see through my window that most people were drifting across to the dining hall. There was no reason that I could think of why anyone should want to summon me then with such urgency. The rapping had made me jump and caused me to feel anxious as well as a mite irritated, which was why I pulled the door open with such vigour. 'Tank!' I said, surprised to find my giant pal standing there. 'Is there a fire?'

'I got it,' he said, ignoring my sarcasm. My eyes flicked to the sheet of paper in his left hand and I knew straight away that he was talking about his parole. Passing me the memo he added, 'I'm out next week.'

After a glance at the paper I shook his other hand and gave him my warmest congratulations, but it was hard to tell from the look on his big face whether he was excited about his result, or worried.

Later, when we talked, it turned out to be a bit of both. I remembered that he had said ages ago he was apprehensive about his eventual release from prison. In fact, when I thought about it, I recalled that he had voiced such concerns on more than one occasion over the past year or so. I hadn't picked him up on it before. I think that was because, at the time, it never came across to me as a real worry. He had mentioned it in passing, when we walked in the prison grounds or worked out in the gym. No more than that, I believed. I mean, how could anyone be worried about being released from prison?

That was what I used to think – before I had experienced what it's like to be near the end of a prison sentence. I once read a news report about a man who had served fifteen years before being transferred to a prison hostel (a kind of halfway house where prisoners are allowed out to work, much the same as I am here) in preparation for his release. He had only been there six weeks when they found him in a local park hanging by the neck from the branch of a tree. The idea of freedom after so long had been too much for him, apparently.

For a long time this story remained a puzzle to me. Because I hardly ever knew or saw anyone who was released from the high-security system, the idea of being freed was only ever a wonderful fantasy. In reality, getting out of prison can be almost as traumatic for some people as coming in – if not more so. But it was hard to see my pal, the man with the biggest heart in the jail, expressing any measure of fear about the prospect of his return to the outside world.

'The thing is,' said Tank as we strolled around the football pitch that evening, 'being in prison for these three years has given me a bit of a break.' He spoke about the problems he had experienced after he left the army: relationship troubles, a custody battle for his little girl, financial worries, and finally the plane trip that was supposed to solve everything, but which had led instead to this stint of imprisonment. He said he really was happy to be getting out at last. But a lot of the problems he had left behind were still out there waiting for him.

'At least I've stopped smoking,' he said. Quite an achievement for someone in prison. 'And I've lost three stone.' Even in the relatively short time I had known him I had seen a significant improvement in his fitness. 'I've done lots of thinking so that I feel confident I can manage my problems out there now, without doing anything drastic.'

It sounded like he was thinking out loud, testing out his appraisal of his situation on me. I was content to just nod in the right places and let him talk. From what I knew of him, exposing his vulnerability in this way was not something Tank did very often. I felt honoured. 'Thank God I got that HGV licence,' he said. I nodded vigorously. 'Got a good job. Probation have got me a flat. Everything's going to be fine.'

I didn't see him again until the end of the week. Before setting off for work I knocked on his door. It was half an hour before he was due for discharge. I heard a muffled 'Yo,' and went in. The big man was still under the covers.

'Good luck, Amigo,' I said and shook his outstretched hand for the last time. He yawned and said 'Thanks.' Then I closed the door and left him. I considered passing on my good advice, but seeing how downbeat he was about getting out somehow it didn't seem appropriate. But everything will be fine. I'm sure of it.

5 June 2003

I'm Cody and I'm innocent!

Make or break time is approaching fast for our friend Cody. After twenty-four years protesting his innocence in prison and eighteen months on bail, his case is listed to be heard at the Court of Appeal next month. His chances look good, it has to be said. Decisions to let life-sentence prisoners out on bail are not taken lightly. In fact, lifers who continue to protest their innocence year after year are often considered by the authorities to be more dangerous than those who have admitted their guilt and decided to 'come to terms' with their crimes.

One of the last 'progress reports' prepared by a senior member of staff on Stephen Downing, for instance, concluded that his continued protestations of innocence indicated that he 'still presented a significant risk'. As such, the recommendation was that he remain in the closed-prison system until he'd received further treatment for his 'offending behaviour'. The twenty-seven years he had given of his life until then for a crime he had been convicted of when he was seventeen years old counted for nothing. His release on bail must have confounded the report writers, but, though a bail let-out shows that the case for the prosecution has been severely weakened by the grounds of the appeal, there was still no guarantee that his conviction would be quashed at the hearing a year later.

Take the case of another young lifer I once knew. Following his conviction, he protested his innocence for seven years before being let out on bail pending a fresh appeal. He spent eighteen months at home with his family waiting for the appeal – then lost the case and was shipped straight back to the closed system (where he would have remained into old age had he not eventually admitted his guilt and engaged with the prison regime). You see, you can just never tell with these things.

The best thing Cody has got going for him – apart from the fresh evidence of course – is that he was bailed from an open prison. As a Category D prisoner he was already on his way out.

A couple of years at the most and he would have been freed on life-licence. Since he has been out on bail he has lived quietly in a small flat, bothering no one. He spends his time cooking – a skill he perfected in prison – and scouring car-boot sales, which didn't exist before he was sent away. He visits his grown-up children and grandchildren regularly and if you passed him in the street I doubt you would give him a second glance. Just an elderly gent going about his business. That's what he looked like when I saw him the other week.

He had dropped me a line and mentioned that he had to see a specialist about the surgery he had undergone while in prison. I phoned him straight away and told him that the hospital he was to attend was just around the corner from where I work. 'Let's meet for coffee,' I suggested.

We timed the meeting for my lunch break. The last time we had seen each other had been in the prison exercise yard along with Felix the Gambler and Big Rinty. Cody had been frail then after his bowel operation. A fifteen-stone man transformed into an eight-stone skeleton in a matter of weeks. How we felt for him – and how we rejoiced when he got bail. Felix wrote to me last year after Cody had visited him in jail and said our ageing pal looked so poorly he didn't think he was going to make it to his appeal.

Immaculate in grey slacks and navy blazer, Cody was sitting at a pavement table when I arrived for our coffee meeting. Up close I noticed the regimental badge on his breast pocket. 'Oi,' I said. He looked up and, beaming his best Cody smile, said, 'Ellow saan.' Then he stood up and we hugged.

There was so much to talk about but so little time. 'You look really well,' I said – and he did. We talked about the old times. The old times? I hadn't realized it was possible to feel nostalgic about time spent in high-security prisons. My break time was over too soon, but I'd got him a present: a peaked cap I'd bought in a novelty shop. The man behind the counter had stamped some words on the front of the cap for me.

'Here,' I said, 'a good-luck token for the appeal.' He took the hat out of the carrier bag and laughed out loud when he read the message. He pulled the cap over his grey hair and we hugged again before parting. 'I'll wear this in court,' he said. I smiled all the way back to the office.

And the message on the hat? What else could it be but, 'I'm Cody, and I'm innocent!'

12 June 2003

Time to go for Frank the Cook

Bad news this week. I've learned that Frank, the prison cook, is due to retire soon. He's done his thirty years and now the time has almost come when he must hang up his oven gloves for good.

The news seemed unbelievable at first. I don't know how old Frank was when he started in the job but he doesn't look anywhere near retirement age. When he told me last weekend while we chatted in the kitchen (as an 'early starter' I was there to collect the cereals and long-life milk for my following week's breakfasts), I took a discreet peek as he turned his head but struggled to spot more than just a few grey hairs among those poking out from beneath his gleaming white trilby hat. 'I don't want to go,' he said, 'but they've told me I don't have a choice.'

How unfair, I thought, that somebody who obviously loves his job so much should be forced to retire. And there is no doubting that Frank does love his job. Everybody here knows it. Anyone who has ever sampled his 'dish of the day' would attest to it.

The quality of the food that Frank prepares is such that even official visitors to the jail are happy not only to queue up with the prisoners in the dining hall to receive it, but also to pay for the privilege. For Frank is a man who believes a taste bud is a taste bud is a taste bud. He does not discriminate between common man and convict. He is simply a cook who delights in giving pleasure to the palate, joy to the juices and satisfaction to the stomach. (A rare bird indeed in a prison kitchen.) 'Food is the sustainer of life,' he told me once. 'It deserves serious attention: in the preparation, in the presentation and in the eating. If you don't get the first two right, the third becomes little more than a mechanical exercise. Food is a hell of a lot more than just fuel, you know?' he went on. 'It's art and it's science. We're lucky in this country to have so much of it – which is why we should always treat it with the greatest of respect.'

Frank is the only prison cook I've ever seen who is happy to stand behind the hotplate at meal times and serve the food he is responsible for preparing. The delicate manner in which he scoops portions of moussaka, special fried rice or beef plate pie before arranging it on to your plate and passing it back to you is something to behold. It beats the usual 'splat! splat! splat!' you come to expect from fellow prisoners who normally man the hotplates, that's for sure.

Food is a huge preoccupation in prison. The anticipation of it: meal times help to break up the monotony. The anxiety it creates: is it going to be hot? Is it going to be cold? Is it going to be edible? The disappointment it so often generates. It may be easy to think of people in the world who are more deserving of decent, well-prepared food than those who end up in prison. But the budget for a prisoner's dietary requirements has barely altered in years and is hardly a sum that a reasonable person would begrudge an incarcerate. Despite this, there is no denying that prison food has improved. The amount of choice has increased dramatically, as have standards of hygiene. But in most establishments it still leaves an enormous amount to be desired. And, while I appreciate that Frank is a special individual, he is not a magician. He is allocated exactly the same resources as every other prison cook. If he can have the effect that he does, why is it that so many others are unable to get close to his standards, let alone match him? Frank might well argue that it is 'art and science'. But it's not rocket science. He's going to be sorely missed.

19 June 2003

Another delay for the Celtic Poet

I'm feeling for the Celtic Poet at the moment. He's had a couple of setbacks and is feeling a little let down. However, I'm sure being in this prison has made it easier to deal with. It's still a penal institution but, with absurdities and irrationalities kept to a minimum, it's nearer to real life than anything we ever encountered in the closed system.

The Poet and I have been here now for about the same length of time, and both of us look a lot healthier than we did when we first landed. I noticed it in him when he started his unescorted outside community work in a local wildlife reserve. Come rain, hail or shine he'd be out on his rebuilt mountain bike first thing in the morning and, with his rucksack on his back and long hair and beard flowing, away he'd pedal.

One or two of the younger, short-term lads started calling him the tree-hugger, but he didn't mind. He was never embarrassed to admit to his love for trees, and after sixteen years away from their company who could blame him if, when he finds himself in the middle of a forest, he gets an uncontrollable urge to hug a few?

During our walks in the evenings he'd tell me about his forest, describing the lichens he'd find as he cleared debris and the way the animals began to emerge and watch him work once they got used to him being around. And it was good to see him looking satisfyingly tired at the end of each day from manual work and fresh air, instead of the weary look from constant psychological conflict.

The physical effect on my pal was most noticeable at the weekends. Witnessing his renewed vitality was like watching a long-dormant flower at last feeling brave enough to unfold its petals. For the first time in all the years I'd known him I saw colour in the Poet's cheeks.

I thought he might wane a little when he got his paid job as a dispatcher in a warehouse. Instead I saw him grow even more confident as his plans became concrete. He started saving his money so he could pay for college courses in forestry and the environment. Because I was a few weeks behind him in my resettlement schedule it felt sometimes like I was hanging on the Poet's shirt-tails, feeling inspired by each progressive step he made. When I started going out of the gate on my own, my hairy friend was around to offer support. When I started paid work, he wanted to know all about it.

Our talks at the weekend continued and I think we were both thankful to have someone close enough to be able to share all these new experiences with. Sometimes we'd look at each other in amazement, both wondering how we'd managed to do it – to have got this far with most of mind and body still intact. The Poet would utter his favourite word, 'Phenomenal,' and I'd shake my head and agree.

For all the uncertain pleasures, however, neither one of us is taking this stage in our respective life sentences lightly. We've been given opportunities and it's up to us to use them. So far so good, you might think – well, not quite.

If all had gone according to plan the Poet should have been a free man by now. At the beginning of the year he was told that his file would be in front of the parole board in March when his case for release would be considered. It was a hearing that was already way overdue. The Poet's tariff (the part of the life sentence that must be served in custody to meet the requirements of 'retribution and deterrence') was up two years ago. The only reason he went over tariff, as far as I can see, is that he occasionally rubbed some of the people in charge of him up the wrong way.

His habit of standing his ground on points of principle did little to endear him to those in authority in the old days. But being a driving force in the creative life of every prison he was ever in should have more than compensated. Producing, directing and performing in plays and self-penned dialogues in prison gyms and chapels, he helped inject desperately needed positive energy into the lives of his fellow prisoners.

But that's another story I suppose. The fact is the Poet's most important parole hearing so far was postponed. Two months, they said. 'There's a new system in place,' explained the governor. 'It's having teething troubles.' In May it was delayed again. 'Your file was misplaced,' he was told, 'but it's been located. Your review will now take place in June.' The board should have sat a couple of days ago. Except a couple of days earlier he received a memo, 'Due to unforeseen circumstances your parole hearing has been postponed for fourteen days.'

26 June 2003

Henry keeps quiet

There are many perks available to a person serving time in open conditions, but none more valuable than the opportunity to go out to paid work. I'm not just talking about the money either – important though that is. I'm thinking more about the whole experience of going to work: getting up in the morning when the alarm goes off, the wake-up shower, choosing which clothes to wear, snatching a quick breakfast before the journey. Once you've been let out through the gate to join the throng there's nobody on your back. If you want, you can pop into a newsagent's and buy yourself a newspaper – any newspaper you choose. If there's time you might even sit in a café for ten minutes and enjoy a morning latte while you browse the headlines.

On arrival at the workplace you can engage with colleagues – chat about the weather or the latest big sporting event – before getting on with the task in hand. Whatever the job, the chances are that you will be left with a sense of satisfaction when the day's labour is over, content in the knowledge that you did your bit. All being well, a decent night's sleep will follow.

I suspect that to the average worker on the outside these activities might appear banal and inconsequential. For the average prisoner, however, it doesn't take many hours of being locked behind a cell door before they become the stuff that dreams are made of.

Easy to imagine then that once paid work has been experienced by someone in prison there would be some reluctance to give it up prematurely. That's probably why most serving prisoners who work on the outside make such good employees. With money to save, as well as the freedom, the responsibility (which helps to bolster a person's sense of dignity like nothing else) and the sweet taste of respectability to savour, there is just too much at stake not to make the effort to shine as an exemplary member of the outside workforce. But there is nothing you can do if you lose your job through no fault of your own – the way Henry did the other month, for example.

It was a shame really. There was no controversy. It wasn't a sacking or a resignation. All that happened was that due to mounting debts the company Henry worked for had to 'downsize' as part of a cost-cutting exercise. They had to lose a dozen workers from the shopfloor, the foreman explained. The last to arrive would be the first to go. With just four months of service to his name Henry found himself at the top of the list for redundancy.

There would have been no black mark if Henry had explained all this to the prison authorities. He had done nothing wrong – not yet anyway. These things happen in real life. But then Henry decided to enter into the realms of make-believe. When he was given his notice he kept the information to himself.

For a full month he went through the motions of getting up early and going to work. Each morning he continued to shower in his usual slot two cubicles down from the one I use. (Prisoners are notorious creatures of habit – and terribly territorial.) I would arrive at 5.45am precisely. Two minutes later Henry would enter the room, his portly form draped in a multi-coloured robe, towel and shampoo in one hand, soap in the other. 'Mornin' Henry,' I'd call from beneath the flow as he strolled past me. Without turning his head he would glance sleepy-eyed in my direction and mutter, 'Mornin'.'

I don't think we ever had more than three proper conversations in the eleven months he was here. All I learned about

Henry was that he was in his late fifties, he was serving four years, on the out he bred budgies – and he was always last in the prison van for our morning ride to the train station (a habit which also continued throughout the month he pretended to go to work).

We're not sure who snitched on Henry, that's if he was snitched on. But Dick the admin orderly said he overheard a governor telling an officer that Henry had said that during his month of pretence he would get off the train a stop earlier than his usual one and would spend all day in the park, or the library, or just mooching outside shop windows until it was time to return to the prison. 'He told the governor he was lucky to get the factory job,' explained Dick. He believed he was too old to get another, apparently, and decided simply to enjoy some extra days out while he had the chance.

Henry's fate was inevitable after that. Last week he was hand-cuffed and driven back to a closed prison. Back to life on the landings and dreaming once more behind a closed cell door.

3 July 2003

Acceptance

Working for a living for the past eight months has been a great experience: getting up in the morning with a real sense of purpose; commuting on the train (I'm an uncommonly happy commuter); striding shoulder to shoulder with members of the public as we make our way to our respective workplaces; and, of course, picking up my pay cheque at the end of each month. It is an odd existence in many ways, like living two lives – partly in, partly out. It's often frustrating, but more often satisfying, and every week that passes I feel more assured that I've done my time in jail the right way.

It helps that the office where I work as an information proces-sor is staffed by people who have been prepared to welcome me as a colleague. Almost two decades of constantly trying to predict actions and reactions (over-analysing conversations, straining to

59

read minds and interpret facial expressions and body language) has left me acutely sensitive to the attitudes and motivations of others. Yet not a single day at work has passed when I have not been made to feel like a valuable member of the team.

It is difficult to quantify the effect this has had on my gradual transition from convict to citizen. In many ways the effect is immeasurable. At the end of my first appraisal by the office manager a little while ago, I made a clumsy attempt to express how important my assimilation into the organization had been in assisting my re-emergence into society.

'Coming out into the free world was more daunting than I anticipated,' I said. 'But the way that you and the other staff have treated me as an equal from the very start has done so much for my confidence out here.'

She was surprised, I think, that there was ever any question about my 'confidence'. But it was not self-confidence that I had in mind. I was talking about the confidence it has taken to operate in this strange land and to function in this new character. 'You fitted straight in,' she said. 'You work well and we're lucky to have you.'

There it was again: that total acceptance of me for who I am and what I can bring to the table – no more, no less. Humbling, but at the same time strengthening.

If anyone was ever to ask me, 'What aspect of your imprisonment has had the most influence on the way you developed while inside?', my answer would be unequivocal. 'Acceptance.'

It sounds simple enough, but acceptance in the manner I'm describing is not something that generally happens in prison. For most prisoners, life on a prison wing seems to consist of one long relationship with rejection and vilification. Staff condemn prisoners. Prisoners condemn each other. (People judge each other in prison more harshly than in any court.) Most guilty people who go to prison don't need reminding how badly they have let others down, or how much they have let themselves down. Most know how much pain and distress their actions have probably caused. It might not always be evident, but most also feel deep shame and embarrassment for having done the deeds that brought them to prison.

To survive on the landings, however, all such feelings must be kept hidden – well hidden. It is only when we encounter people who are prepared to accept us for who we are that we can be honest about ourselves. And without honesty very little real development is possible. I have been fortunate to meet some special, accepting people during my years of imprisonment. They will never be forgotten. But before I started being let out of the prison gate on my own I hadn't considered that acceptance on the outside would be an issue. Not until I experienced it. Then I wondered how I would ever have managed without it. For rejection and vilification have far more potential to debilitate on the outside. That was why I felt so compelled to explain to the office manager about the added benefits my job has brought. I needed her to know.

10 July 2003

The legend of Felton's flask bomb

Felton Leaky was a name I first heard being bandied around soon after arriving at my first high-security prison. He had obviously been quite a character in the place. Whenever he had had to be taken 'down the block' for example (the punishment block or segregation unit) it had always taken several prison officers in full riot gear (the mufti squad) to get him down there. But apparently he was not a big man, nor was he a hard-man in the traditional prison sense.

People I spoke to said Felton, a lifer, had never presented any sort of threat to his fellow prisoners. It was clear that many were wary of him due to the way he fearlessly confronted prison officers any time he felt that his rights were being infringed. But just as many admired him for it – gaining vicarious satisfaction whenever he was at full rant in the office, and enjoying seeing the men with the keys on the defensive, being reminded that they were only in control because of the 'goodwill' of most of the prisoners.

The truth is that few prisoners really want trouble with staff. Most just want to 'do their bird' and get back out again. Sadly, doing time is rarely that simple. Too many unnecessary obstacles, too many no's for no good reason. So the reasonable people bite their lips when the frustration levels are at their highest – and revel quietly in the activities of men like Felton.

I had missed him by a couple of weeks. He had been shipped out after his last altercation with officers – though 'altercation' hardly does justice to the event in question. After removing the vacuum capsule from his thermos flask, he had filled it with a pound or two of his own excrement before marching purpose-fully with it in the direction of the wing office, where four prison officers were enjoying their tea break. Nobody knew for sure what was the cause of Felton's latest gripe. If they did, it was for-gotten in the incident's aftermath. It must have been something he felt particularly strongly about, however.

When Felton stepped inside the small, glass-panelled room, the officers, who were all sitting around the desk, looked up briefly before returning to their newspapers and diaries. The senior office in charge told Felton to come back later. 'Can't you see we're having our tea?' he said grumpily, it was reported.

'This'll only take a moment,' said Felton, and then launched his shiny grenade at the ceiling directly above the desk, before hightailing it back down the landing. The effect of the explosion can only be imagined. Not surprisingly the splattered officers vacated the office in a rapid and distressed manner. According to witnesses the effect was reminiscent of a scene from a disaster movie set in a sewage plant. (I was sceptical about the number of people who claimed to have actually seen the action take place. It generated so much excitement on the wing that it appeared to have sparked off an episode of 'I-was-there' syndrome.)

There was a price to be paid. Everyone out on the landing was quickly banged up so that the perpetrator could safely be removed from the wing. The screams that were heard coming from the block that night were assumed to have been Felton's, though nobody could say for sure as the next day he was gone. The governor who signed the ship-out ticket vowed that Felton would never set foot in his prison again. The con who worked as the reception orderly reported that Felton just smiled and began singing, 'Goodbyee, goodbyee...'

I heard Felton's name on the grapevine many times over the following years: rooftop protests, cell barricades, more instances of 'shitting up' prison staff (using a variety of methods). His reputation in the system achieved legendary proportions. But I had never met him in person until last weekend.

I had learned he was in the jail the previous week from Pete, the new prison van driver. On the way back from the station that night the conversation among the lads in the van was all about Felton. His arrival seemed to cause anticipation and anxiety in equal measure, but our paths didn't cross until the following Sunday morning.

I was leaving the laundry room as he was going in. Not knowing what he looked like, I didn't know it was him at the time. 'Mornin',' he said, nodding as we passed each other. 'Mornin'' I replied. When Felton was pointed out to me later I was stunned. He looked so ordinary.

17 July 2003

The Poet's day comes

There was something majestic about the way the Celtic Poet walked towards the gatehouse last Friday morning. As he moved, his long chestnut hair (still almost free of grey, despite more than sixteen years in prison) seemed to bob in slow motion with every step. His dress was low-key and typical of the Poet's style: new sand-coloured walking boots, 'a bargain from the Army and Navy store', olive-green cargo pants and an open tartan shirt over a brilliant white vest. But with his head tipped ever so slightly back, he looked taller, I thought – and more dignified than usual.

We had said our goodbyes only moments earlier. It had been a brief farewell. 'Take care, friend,' I said, as we shook hands. 'You too,' he said. 'It'll be your turn before you know it.' Then he picked up his rucksack, slung it over his shoulder and set off across the tarmac for the last time. The sun had barely risen in the clear blue sky and it cast a long shadow behind my pal's lean frame. I stepped back inside and watched from a ground-floor window as he took his final steps to freedom. When he reached the steel grill in the fence and pressed the bell, I turned away and returned to my room. I knew he wouldn't look back.

The Poet once described the prison system to me as 'a multi-chambered sarcophagus'. He said it was filled with 'ghosts, visitors and walking dead people'. At the time I don't think either of us were sure in which category we were. In the middle stages of our life sentences then (although I was three years ahead), we were both still learning and growing and living on a high-security wing that had been specially built to house a hundred life-sentence prisoners. When it was opened, somebody wrote Death Row above the entrance. Nobody ever bothered to erase it.

They were intense times. The irony is that prison officers will often say that they prefer 'working with lifers'. Many staff will jump at the chance to supervise 'lifer wings'. While it's true that lifers are generally more compliant and less troublesome to 'work with', relations between such prisoners, away from official eyes, are in fact complicated and finely balanced.

Life on the specially designated wings can be the most demanding. Having to spend what can seem an eternity exposed on prison landings with the same people month after month, year after year, hones the survival instinct so much that senses become fixed in a state of high alert and nerves stay constantly taut. Fear and anticipation of violence shadows every interaction. You long to be able to trust your neighbour, but you dare not. You hope that your conversations are honest – but you're never sure. And all the time you're trying to hang on to what was left of your humanity when you entered the system.

That was one of the main strengths of the Poet in those days.

I don't think he was aware of it, but he had the type of character that was interpreted by those around him as neutral. Out on the landings he was a natural, calming influence in a psychological maelstrom. His presence in the music group or the drama class acted as a cohesive force. He was held in high esteem. We could talk about him openly and with no fear of comebacks (like the time we ribbed him when he played Mephistopheles in a production of *Dr Faustus* and he was the only member of the cast who did not have to be made up). For the Poet was common ground.

It wasn't always like that for the bearded one, of course. The Poet did not know what he had to offer when he first came to prison. He would be the first to admit that his gifts were hidden deep – even from himself. One of the reasons he and I became acquainted all those years ago, I'm sure, was because we both looked upon the prison experience as a voyage of self-discovery. We didn't tell each other that. It was something we sensed, I think. The two of us did not really become friends until this last year or so together in open conditions. But looking back I can recall appreciating the Poet's presence in that unnatural environment. Even in prison no man is an island. Wherever we are, we need to see elements of ourselves reflected in others. If we're fortunate we see those elements in people that we can respect and from whom we can learn. I'm glad I knew the Celtic Poet – and grateful for what I learned from him.

24 July 2003

I believe Cody

Whatever anyone else might think, I've made my mind up. If the truth be known I think I made it up a while ago – several years ago in fact – but it didn't feel safe to admit it then, not even to myself.

You hear so many excuses in prison, so many tales. When it comes to questions of innocence or guilt you learn to listen to the stories of fellow prisoners with a sceptical ear, for it is too dangerous to allow yourself to be persuaded. The stakes are too high. You choose to disbelieve one man only to see him walk free from the Court of Appeal, exonerated after he's done a fifteen or twenty stretch. You believe another – then the appeal-court judges test the case afresh with new evidence and once again he is condemned.

So if you're wise and you want to retain your ability to reason effectively you should avoid taking a view in such cases. Take people as you find them and hope they do the same with you. That's always been my philosophy on the subject anyway – except I'm not always true to it. As in the case of Cody, for example. When I heard the other week that his appeal hearing had been postponed until the autumn, I jumped down off the fence immediately. If anyone had asked at that moment I'd have told them straight – loud and clear. I wanted to shout it from the rooftops, 'CODY IS INNOCENT!'

We spoke about his appeal the week before the hearing was due to take place. I'd called him on his mobile phone and asked him how he was feeling about his appearance in court. 'I'm fine about it,' he said, 'I'm dying to get in there.' There was no trace of anxiety or nerves in his voice. Even though he's been waiting for it for twenty-four years, his answers were very matter of fact. 'I just want to get it over with,' he said. 'One way or the other.'

One way or the other. That was the rub. For all our optimism (many people across the whole prison system know about Cody's case and most of those who know him are rooting for him) there was always the possibility that his appeal would fail. If that happened our pal would be sent straight back to prison. High-security first, for allocation – then back to open conditions where he was when he was let out on bail. But it would be no consolation, for him or his loved ones.

When we were in the closed system – me, Felix the Gambler and Big Rinty – we often discussed Cody's case. He'd shown us the paperwork. There were anomalies: things that didn't add up in the prosecution's argument; contradicting witness statements, dates and times that did not correspond. But much as we cared for him I do not recall any of us voicing a view about the legitimacy of his conviction. 'The only person who knows the truth,' opined Felix the Gambler one day as we walked in the exercise yard, 'is Cody himself.'

We just wanted him to get a result and get out, because, like nearly everyone in those places then (apart from a few prison officers), we liked and respected him and believed he'd done enough time. I never knew the private views of the others, but only at night before sleep – the time reserved for serious thinking – did I ever consider Cody's situation in any depth. What if he really was innocent, I'd wonder. It was a difficult question. All those years away from home. His young children grown to adults without him. If he was telling the truth, every day an enormous crime was being committed against him and his family.

I remember when he returned from the outside hospital after his life-saving surgery for a bowel condition that prison medical staff had missed. He had lost seven stone and looked like a walking skeleton. Because of his surgical wounds the hospital had given him baggy tracksuit bottoms to wear. He explained to the reception officer he needed baggy prison clothes. 'You'll get what I fucking give you,' said the officer. I was there. I saw and heard it. Inside I boiled with anger. Cody was weak and vulnerable, but he managed to respond. 'I hope you remember that when I walk out of the Court of Appeal.'

I know it will happen. We'll just have to wait a little longer.

31 July 2003

Kelty

'Blade for hire.' That was how fellow YOs described Kelty during his time in the YOIs (young offenders' institutions). Serving HMP (Her Majesty's pleasure: a life sentence for the under-eighteens), Kelty was in the young-offender system for four years before he was 'starred up' at the age of twenty-one and transferred to the adult system. According to the Kid he managed the move well enough. He and Kelty had known each other in the YOIs but had never been friends. Kelty was 'too leery', the Kid explained. 'He was too jumpy, always trying to impress.'

The Kid was in the YO system for five years before he was starred up. He'd used his time there constructively – education, sports, drama, charity events – but he'd had his moments too, not least of which was his spectacular escape and the two weeks he spent 'at large' when he'd barely turned seventeen, which made the headlines. It gave him a big reputation after his recapture, but the Kid did his best to play it down. 'It was weird,' he told me, 'once I was back in, I was getting all kinds of respect, even from the older lads. But the truth was, the escape was a panic reaction. As soon as I was out there again I panicked even more. I couldn't handle it. I'd already decided to hand myself in when the police picked me up.'

After he was recaptured he settled down and decided that he was going to make prison work for him. Being honest with himself was the first and biggest step he had to take. 'I didn't want to be a play-actor anymore,' he told me. 'I wanted to be a real person.'

How anybody comes to such a decision in prison is still a mystery to me. But lucky for him it happened and as far as I can tell, he never looked back. So when he landed in the adult system he had a good understanding of who he was and where he wanted to go. Unlike Kelty, still play-acting and glorying in his role as a hired chib man.

It would be easy to condemn Kelty for his attitude and early prison behaviour. But to appreciate his position you would have to look at his situation through his eyes – and from inside his skin. YOIs are not children's homes or boarding schools. They are hostile institutions. Most of the young people who inhabit them have long since been damaged by emotional neglect or adverse formative experiences at the hands of elders or those who should have been their protectors. For all the help and support available to young prisoners, many problematic characteristics are so deeply rooted in troubled early lives that it is a wonder any of the youngsters are ever able to see time spent in a YOI as a beneficial or meaningful experience. The fortunate ones, like the Kid, mature early and, with the right support and guidance, can step back to see how best to take advantage of their disadvantage. But for every YO like the Kid there are a hundred like Kelty.

It wasn't the age difference that kept Kelty and me from ever having a conversation of more than five minutes. Before I knew anything about him we spoke on the landing shortly after I arrived. He told me that he had been 'grounded' for some misdemeanour. Tall and skinny, with a sharp face and small blue eyes, I thought he was in his early twenties until the Kid enlightened me. We became nodding acquaintances. 'How's it going?' I'd ask. 'Sweet,' Kelty would reply. We never really got much further.

I never really felt sorry for him. Once I knew his history I knew he would never move forward until that thing happened inside his head – the way it had happened to the Kid so many years earlier. The night before the Kid was released last year, a few of us gathered in his room to drink his coffee and wish him well. Kelty came to the door and the Kid invited him in. Kelty's tariff had been up years before the Kid's but all the 'blade for hire' foolery had kept him in. He sat in the corner and didn't say very much.

I haven't seen Kelty for a while now, but I know he's moving forward at last. In a couple of weeks the prison is hosting an afternoon of games and fun activities for local young people with learning disabilities. I saw the notice on the board at the gatehouse. Kelty is down as one of the organizers.

7 August 2003

Commuter conflict

You know, I've had some lovely train journeys. Even after more than a year of weekday commuting by rail I still thrill at the glimpses of the countryside through the grimy windows – and with no bars, doors, walls or fences to obstruct the views, I marvel at being able to see for miles into the distance. However, despite this taste of liberty that I've been allowed to enjoy so far – and it has been a most generous helping – I take nothing for granted.

The time I spend on the train, going to and from work, has become my time for reflection and contemplation. Apart from the odd mobile-phone conversation and the sound of the wheels on the track, it is a very quiet journey. I'm well used to that now: the lack of acknowledgement. I've learned commuter etiquette: shuffle up, keep feet tucked in, avoid eye-contact. All in all, ideal conditions in which to simply sit and think and, along with nearly everyone else, mind my own business.

I've had a good run, I suppose. More than a year of almost incident-free commuting. Incredible when you consider the scale of the personal-space invasion that takes place each day. But it reached a new level of intensity on my train the other morning.

We had been warned. The message that flashed up on the screen above the hatch in the ticket office was clear, 'Please note, this train is only eight coaches long.' I wasn't sure how many coaches there normally were, but as soon as I boarded I noticed it was much more crowded than usual. I took one of the few remaining seats – an empty double – and sat in the space farthest from the window. A couple of stops later and it was standing room only.

The spot beside me remained untaken. Another couple of stops and the aisles were packed shoulder to shoulder. The place next to me must have been the last available in the carriage. Still no takers. Then I saw the commotion. Someone was forcing their way along the crowded aisle. A pointless exercise, I thought. The intrepid passenger thought otherwise. When he came into view I felt my heart rate quicken. He carried a holdall over his shoulder – as well as a briefcase in one hand and a newspaper in the other – and he had his eyes trained on the seat next to mine. Throughout his struggle to pass the static bodies, I had heard not a single 'excuse me'. That made me nervous.

He collapsed into the space and immediately set about organizing his accoutrements. The holdall went by his feet. He opened his briefcase and drew out a laptop and two mobile phones and began to spread himself out. I leaned over into the aisle. This was a man whose need for space was greater than mine. I closed my eyes and thought about prison.

It was only minutes later when I felt the pressure against my ribs. At first I thought I was imagining it. The point of an elbow? It couldn't be, surely. But it was.

I leaned farther away. Soon my back was hurting. Hang on a minute, I thought. I've paid the same as him for this seat. I was entitled to sit up straight. So I did. Back came the elbow. I wasn't budging. And so battle commenced.

A glance at his computer revealed little activity. He was obviously too preoccupied with trying to make me budge. I was determined to resist this blatant act of aggression. I couldn't help thinking it would never happen in prison – not without ensuing combat. I thought about my pal Toby Turner. This laptop lout was lucky he wasn't sitting next to him in his heyday. I could just imagine Toby's reaction to the elbow treatment.

Paying no heed to the mass of silent bystanders, my shaven-headed friend would have been on his feet in a flash. 'Do you know how many fuckin' anger-management courses I've done?'

'Er, no,' his startled tormentor would stutter.

'Six fuckers!' Toby would yell. 'And I still ain't passed!'

In spite of the increased elbow pressure from my odd travelling companion, my mental image of him being subjected to one of Toby's tantrums was making me smile.

However, it was time to bring this silliness to an end. Leaning away again, I stood up slowly. The next station was at least twenty-five minutes away. He turned his head. I bent towards him. 'There you go,' I said, almost whispering. 'You obviously want my seat too. Well, it's all yours.'

The passengers closest to us looked over, no doubt curious. His face reddened. I felt for him, but what else could I have done? As I said, I've had some lovely train journeys. That wasn't one of them.

14 August 2003

Where is Tank?

It's hard to believe that almost three months have passed since Tank was released. I thought about him on and off for a while afterwards – just brief moments of wondering, hoping that things were panning out for him. Even though you get close to people in prison, you learn never to become too attached or dependent.

That's what I have learned over the years anyway. Overnight a person you considered a friend can quite easily turn into your mortal enemy. Another whose companionship you enjoyed is shipped out unexpectedly or is discharged, or worse.

So you get used to being self-reliant, never kidding yourself that any friendships you might form with fellow prisoners will ever be anything other than temporary acquaintance. But it would take the hardest of hearts to forget people altogether.

I still get a lift whenever I return to my room at night and find a letter from Big Rinty or Felix the Gambler. Or a card from Cody giving me the latest on his appeal prospects. We shared powerful times in our lives, making emotional connections in the process. The giving and receiving of unconditional support and encouragement when the going is tough can be profoundly meaningful. But deep down we are never in any doubt that so long as we're in prison, we stand or fall alone.

To tell the truth, I had not expected to hear from Tank again. It concerned me that he was still in bed half an hour before he was due to walk out of the gate on the Friday morning that we shook hands and said our farewells. I knew he was anxious about returning to life outside. But he had a good job as a lorry driv-er. He had somewhere to live. And, best of all, he had a clear head – a better set of circumstances than most people getting out of prison these days.

I missed him for a while. There was a big space in the gym whenever I made the effort to get myself down there. Tank was my workout partner and without him around I found I was attending fewer PE sessions on my days in.

When I did go, I noticed it was quieter without the big man's funny banter and without his lion-like roar whenever he was going for his bench press personal best. For weeks it was hard to get motivated for the gym. Tank's departure totally messed up my training routine. I had to dig a little deeper than usual but I recovered my stride eventually.

I have to say it was good to hear so many nice things being said about my big pal after he had gone. It became clear that he was genuinely well thought of both by members of staff and fellow prisoners. Every other day it seemed I was getting asked if I had heard from him.

'He was a top man.'

'He was a good neighbour.'

'He would help anybody.'

'Have you heard from him yet? Give him my regards if you write to him.'

This last accompanied nearly every interaction I had when the big man's name came into the conversation. But the weeks passed and there was never any word. I didn't feel bad about that. If he wanted to draw a line under his prison time and all that went with it, well that was more than fair enough with me.

We had a few laughs together. We had some good talks. That was what mattered.

Nevertheless, how pleased I was to find a letter waiting from my Hulk-like chum when I returned from work the other evening. A lovely surprise.

'I hope this letter finds you well and keeping fit...'

Well, not as fit as I was, I thought.

'Life behind the wheel of a truck has taken its toll,' he wrote.

I had warned him about the dangers of a sedentary career.

'I have not gained any weight but lost some tone.'

Mmm.

'Last week on my only day off I went out and bought a set of dumb-bells.'

Good for him.

He explained that he was now driving a big white artic, delivering 'fresh produce all over the isle'.

Easy to imagine him smiling at the traffic lights; tipping his bushman's hat to crossing pedestrians; bantering with the depot foreman.

'Well, good buddy, hope to hear from you soon. A big "Hi" to all the guys there. You take good care. Tank.'

Tank told me once that his father had once told him, 'Son: the road is a healer.' I think his father was right.

21 August 2003

Fun at the fair with Leaky, Larrson and Fartin' Martin

A good day in prison. It may sound like a contradiction in terms, but they do occur, and more regularly than you might imagine. There was one here recently that I think could safely be described as such. A day when the guests of Her Majesty had guests of their own: special guests, with special needs, who arrived by coach in the middle of a sunny morning to take part in the prison's annual 'special events' day.

Preparations had been going on for months. The collection jar had been on the counter of the gatehouse reception hatch since the spring and had yielded a healthy sum in loose change. Pete the prison van driver took on the role of chief organizer. He managed to get hold of all the necessary materials, and organized prisoners and staff to take charge of the sports field activities. Once the bunting was up and the marquees and stalls erected, the perimeter fence was almost unnoticeable. It looked like the setting for a fête that could have been taking place in any village anywhere in the country.

Eyebrows were raised, mind you, and sniggers suppressed

when Felton Leaky was named as the man in charge of the welly-throwing competition. He's only been in the jail a few weeks, but there's nobody here now who has not heard of his anti-authoritarian exploits during his nineteen years in the closed-prison system. Nor are there many who have not baulked at tales of receptacles filled with unsavoury substances being launched in the direction of disobliging members of staff by the fearless one.

On the day, however, Felton performed admirably. There were hecklers at the sidelines as his event began. One shouted, 'Don't forget to check the inside of that thing before you throw it!' But Felton parried them gracefully and concentrated on ensuring that his participants had a constant supply of missiles. He couldn't be faulted for effort. Every time I looked, he was sprinting up and down retrieving ammunition, or lining up alongside a novice thrower, demonstrating the best technique.

The guests were split into groups of half a dozen or so. Chaperoned by care staff, most of whom were young women from their own communities, they were free to wander about and take part in anything that took their fancy.

Larrson was in charge of the tombola. His almost fluorescent green eyes and large shaved head were probably as much of a draw as his soft toys and toiletry prizes. And a very lucky stall it was. Nobody walked away empty-handed.

It was a similar situation at the 'strength hammer'. Jed, whose last stint here was forty years ago (when the prison was a detention centre and he was just fifteen), supervised the game. There must have been a lot of strong individuals having a go, as every time the hammer swung the bell rang out loud and clear.

Relays were popular, organized by PE staff, as were all the minor games: hoop throwing; penalty kicks; skittle swing and one-hit cricket. Kelty excelled in his role as 'sports coach'. His patience and gentle manner as he assisted the guests belied his dangerous history.

Listening to the squeals of glee and laughter that echoed

around the field, along with music from the Cheeky Girls CD, it was hard to believe that any of us were actually still in jail. Given the right set of circumstances, I thought, none of us would have looked out of place at a bank-holiday picnic – not that we'd all make good picnic companions, I remembered. I was thinking particularly of the prisoner who manned the 'Guess My Nickname' stall. This is a man whose reputation for almost preternatural wind-breaking has earned him a sobriquet that rhymes perfectly with his Christian name. 'Me first name's Martin,' he told groups of bemused guests who meandered by. Much to the relief of onlookers in the know he added, 'No more clues.'

Frank the Cook and his team from the kitchen provided a fine buffet lunch. Ice cream was donated by a local company (proceeds from sales of the giant cones went straight into the pot for next year's bash). It was good to see some staff in on their day off too, several of whom had brought their families. A duty governor unsportingly declined an invitation to be locked in the stocks and pelted with wet sponges. ('I've got my best suit on,' he whined.) But all in all, nobody who was present could deny that it really was a very good day in prison.

28 August 2003

The man with the bag

As always, the station platform was crowded when I arrived for my train back to the prison the other evening. It was raining lightly and I was damp from my walk from the office. Since I had a twenty-minute wait, I decided to nip into the platform coffee bar and try to dry off. I grudgingly paid my £1.75 for a lukewarm latte and drew a stool up to the counter by the window. From my position I could see directly across to the platform opposite.

The waiting faces looking back were both familiar and unfamiliar. Many, like me, were regulars – commuters at the end of their working day. Others were obviously returning from shopping trips, or from journeys further afield, perhaps, with bags, cases, holdalls and pushchairs. As I sipped my coffee I scanned the ranks to see if there was anybody I recognized. It's a game I often play when I'm among large crowds. During my almost two decades in prison I must have met thousands upon thousands of people. But I have yet to bump into anybody outside that I knew on the landings.

A train drew in on the other side. Some disembarked, some stepped aboard and a little while later it pulled away. I finished my coffee and was about to wander around to stand at my usual boarding spot when I noticed the man under the canopy on the opposite platform. He was crouched down against a wall. I'd never seen him before in my life. But from that single glance I knew more about him than any stranger ought to know about another.

It wasn't his clothes that gave him away: canvas shoes, denims, checked jacket. And his fair hair was tidy enough, his face clean-shaven. A youngish man, probably in his early thirties, I guessed, he was doing nothing to draw attention to himself. Like any other weary traveller, I thought, he should have been allowed to crouch in pleasant anonymity, keeping his business to himself until he chose to share it.

Instead, his recent past was revealed for the whole world to see. Like a public branding, it was emblazoned in thick capital letters on the large open polythene bag sitting next to him, which appeared to hold all his worldly possessions. Even with four sets of railway tracks between us I could read the print clearly: HM PRISON SERVICE. I've seen so many of those bags, through dozens of transfers and cell moves. But I've never seen one outside the prison context before. It was a depressing sight.

Minutes later, I emerged from the underpass on to the man's platform. As I approached he turned his head up to face me and I half smiled and nodded to reassure him that I presented no threat. He nodded back. Up close I checked that no one else was in earshot and said, 'All right, mate?'

'Er, yeah, thanks,' he said.

Realizing he might be thinking I was up to something dodgy, I added quickly, 'I saw your bag.'

'Eh?' he said.

'Your bag,' I said, nodding again.

'Mmm. Just got out this morning,' he said. 'What's it to you, anyway?'

'I'm still in,' I said. 'I get out through the week to go to work. I'm on my way back. I saw you from across the way. I can't believe they gave you that for your gear.'

'Well, they did,' he said with a mock laugh.

Once he'd relaxed we chatted a little about the system. When I told him I was in a resettlement prison, designed to let people out in stages, he said, 'I could have done with some of that.' He told me that he'd done three years. He was of no fixed abode, but was hoping a relative would allow him to sleep on her settee. That morning the prison had given him £94 and a travel warrant. In his prison bag I noticed some certificates. I saw that one was for completing an anger-management course and another was for getting a negative result on an MDT (mandatory drug test). 'It was work skills I needed,' he said, 'but there's just too many cons waiting for too few places on the vocational training courses. You need to be doing life to get anything worthwhile in there.'

'Mmm,' I said.

While we talked, my train pulled in and left. If I'd missed the next one I'd have been late back for sure and in danger of being declared 'unlawfully at large', so I wished the man well and returned to my own platform. His train pulled in and then he was gone. My train followed and then I was gone, too. I managed to get a seat by a window, but it was an uncomfortable journey. All I could think about was that damned bag.

Whatever the man had done, he'd served his sentence. He didn't deserve that as well.

11 September 2003

The yoga teacher makes Joe smile again

From the off, Joe Fales looked to me like a disillusioned long-term prisoner. His age, mid- to late forties, was an indication that he might have been inside for a while. As was the absence of lustre in his skin and the dullness in his eyes. These I noticed whenever I found myself anywhere near him, usually in the meal queue or reading the papers in the library. But the biggest clue that made me think he was a con who had lost his direction and focus was the way he walked. Whenever I saw him in the grounds, or going back and forth to the dining hall, he appeared to be moving in a way that I can only describe as a sort of purposeless amble – as if it no longer mattered whether or not he got to where he was supposed to be going.

He and I would probably have become acquainted eventually. In such a small community everyone gets to know everyone else in time. But with me out of the prison for much of the week and him still undergoing the induction process, it would have taken a little longer than usual, I think, for the right circumstances to occur. He landed here a few months ago but it was many weeks later before we got to the polite 'All right?' or 'Mornin'' stage whenever we passed each other. There was never any reason to say more, until I received the letter from the yoga teacher.

The letter was a nice surprise. The yoga teacher had brought much peace and harmony to one of the closed prisons in which I had spent some difficult years. His gentle but determined tutoring had introduced a desperately needed method of relaxation to those who attended his class. More than that, he created a venue where case-hardened prisoners could lower defences and communicate in the manner of ordinary people. His respectful attitude encouraged self-respect among his students, reminding us we were human and that it was OK to feel a mite vulnerable occasionally. I'm not sure if he ever realized it, but we took a great deal of what he taught us back to the landings and because of that I believe his good influence radiated in some measure throughout the wings.

The yoga teacher and I stayed in contact after I moved on, but more than a year had passed since we'd been in touch. His latest letter brought catch-up news: his family were well, so was his business (teaching yoga in prisons was something he did voluntarily in his spare time). He finished off with sincere best wishes and then added, 'By the way, have you met Joe Fales yet? I understand he's been transferred to your place. He's doing life and not doing too well.' He wrote that Joe had been a great help in getting the yoga group going in a dour prison in the Midlands.

Until then I hadn't even known Joe's first name. A week or so later I was on my way in to the dining hall as he was coming out. I stepped towards him and said, 'Joe Fales?'

'Yes,' he said.

'We have a mutual friend,' I said. 'The yoga teacher.'

'Oh yes,' he said, smiling broadly. His eyes brightened. 'I knew him in the closed prison I was in before I came here,' he added. 'A gentleman. Helped me though a very dark patch.'

We were soon involved in a full-blown conversation, heaping praise on the yoga teacher and relating how much his teachings had assisted us during times of stress. I have to say, I was taken aback seeing this previously dejected-looking man suddenly become so animated. But I shivered when he told me his story.

Fales had been in a prison like this before. It had taken him fifteen years to get there. He had got a good job, working long hours. One day he returned from work and gave a positive reading on the alcometer. After a period of being grounded he went back to work, but six weeks later he gave another positive test. This time he was told to pack and the next morning he was shipped back to the closed system. It took him four years to get back to open conditions.

It was his own fault, of course. It was grossly foolish to ignore the first warning and he knows it. But I'm struggling to understand what those extra four years achieved. Four years' imprisonment is the equivalent of a six-year prison sentence (with two off for 'good behaviour'). To receive such a sentence, a person must commit a very serious crime. Joe Fales broke prison rules and he had a good idea of the consequences if he got caught out, but I would argue against anyone who said he deserved a six-stretch for it.

18 September 2003

My first (legal) car

A confession: I am now a fully fledged, bona fide, all-legal-and-above-board, er... car owner. Amazing when you think about it, that a person can be in prison and have a car parked legitimately on the other side of the fence for their daily use. It sounds like something you might read about happening in another country. A country perceived to have a more 'progressive' attitude towards crime and punishment. Somewhere such as Sweden or Germany, for example.

For all the difficulties being experienced at present in our prison system, however (a system arguably in a state of crisis), there is still a strong belief among some of those in charge that providing conditions and facilities that will assist prisoners to rehabilitate themselves is the only way of using prison to society's best advantage.

Car ownership must be the ultimate privilege for a prisoner – but it is also the ultimate responsibility. And nothing facilitates rehabilitation like responsibility.

Even though buying a car was the obvious step after passing my test last year, to have reached the stage in my sentence when I am allowed to own a car feels a little unreal. For so many years my only real dream was to stay alive long enough to be able to experience one sunny day on the outside again. It would have been dangerous in those days to wish for any more. But compared to the freedoms I have been allowed to enjoy since landing in open conditions almost two years ago that dream now seems so pathetic. One sunny day? Circumstances must have been pretty dire.

The build-up to the car purchase was long and drawn out. First of all I had to save up the money. Then I had to apply to the activities department for permission. Filling in the application form was easy enough and quite exciting, until I got to the 'previous motoring convictions' box. They wanted offences, dates and punishments. I had so many and it was all so long ago (first court appearance, 1972: driving with no licence, no tax and no insurance). The fact that I now had a spanking new full driving licence without the blemish of even a single penalty point made no difference. They wanted precise details of my entire driving history.

A helpful security governor came up with the official printout list after a bit of research. He gave me a copy and I was embarrassed reading it. The driving record of a young fool.

When I had saved enough to buy a car that I thought should be reasonably reliable, I started combing the small ads of a local freesheet. I had a look at a few before deciding on a seven-year-old Volvo. The seller convinced me with his warm, sincere manner. I had still not got over my problem of thinking that everyone on the outside is honest. 'I bought it for my sister-in-law who was going to learn to drive, but now she's changed her mind.' Sounded plausible. I thought I had a bargain and handed over the cash. Within a week it needed a new starter motor and replacement earth lead connections. Another £300. But you live and learn. It seems to be running smoothly now.

It was my pal Big Rinty who first planted the idea of car ownership in my head. Meeting up with him after he was recalled to prison was heartbreaking in one respect. But he shared with me so much of what he had experienced out there in order to help me when my turn came. He told me about his driving experiences. He had passed his test long before he ever went to prison for life. Soon after getting out he bought a cheap car just so he could 'get the hang of driving again'. He said he had no problems until the day he was stopped by the police. When the young officer in charge asked to see his driving licence Rinty handed over the little red book that had lain in his prison property box for almost twenty years.

'What's this?' asked the officer.

'My licence,' said Rinty.

'Are you serious?' said the officer, beckoning to his colleague.

An escorted trip to the local station followed, where Rinty explained his situation and was instructed in no uncertain terms (once the officers and their colleagues had stopped rolling about laughing) to exchange his licence for its modern equivalent at the earliest opportunity.

'But best of all,' he told me, 'was the drive to the coast.' One day he had taken a packed lunch and driven to a seaside town. After parking near the beach he sat for the whole afternoon just looking out at the sea. 'It was one of my prison dreams come true,' he said.

One of these days I think I'm going to have to drive over and pay my pal a visit.

25 September 2003

A dream visit to the barber's

It was an unhappy day when Binton was discharged from here a few months ago. Not for him, obviously. But for those he left behind who depended on his barbering skills – especially me – it was devastating. Finding a decent barber in prison is never easy. There are plenty of chancers, of course, who will tell you they've 'done training on the out', anything to get their hands on a phonecard – the going rate for a prison haircut. Then you see the results in a mirror and a week's depression follows.

Having said that, a bad haircut in the closed system doesn't matter too much as nobody who really counts is in danger of seeing you for a while. And you can always time the event well before a visit, just to be on the safe side. But here in open conditions when you're venturing into the outside world so often, proper hair-grooming is crucial.

Binton was good. He landed here around the same time as I did. His personal barbering kit had been spotted in reception and word had got around quickly. Within days he had set up shop outside his room in the evenings. You could even book an appointment in advance. And he listened to what you asked for, without prying into your business. When he left, however, I knew I would have to face up to the idea of visiting a civilian barber for the first time in a long while. So long, in fact, that I cannot remember the last time I went for a haircut 'on the out' (although I do recall that it cost around £1).

As soon as I knew for sure that Binton was leaving, I made an extra effort during my outside travels to find somewhere suitable. In vain, I kept my eyes peeled for the red-and-white pole of a traditional comb-and-scissors man. I discovered plenty of 'hair-dressing salons' with names like Toni&Guy. But I was looking for a Mick's, a Dave's, or a Brian's.

Every time I thought I'd found somewhere with a non-threat-ening frontage, it seemed to be staffed mainly by young women. In other circumstances, this might be a pleasing prospect for (ahem) a middle-aged man. When I first went away to prison, my firm young scalp was covered in a mass of dark curls, a thatch that any man would be proud to present to a bevy of manicured maids, but these days – misplaced vanity, I know – I baulk at the thought of a pretty young stranger getting too close to my grey streaks and bald patch.

To be truthful, I'm not that self-conscious about the lack of luscious locks. The running joke between me and Jimmy Jodhpurs – the youngster who did the barbering in the high-security jail I was in when I first noticed that my barnet was being subjected to the law of diminishing returns – went some-thing like this:

Me: 'How's the sunroof looking?' I'd will him to reply 'hairi-er' but he never did. He was too honest.

'Er, it's getting bigger,' he'd say.

'But is there still hair there?'

'Oh yeah,' he'd say, 'a bit.'

My response was always the same, 'Where there's hair there's hope.'

When it goes, it goes – and it's no use getting distressed about it. But that's not the point. Any sensible person would wonder why the big deal, it's only a haircut. And I'd have to agree. A visit to a proper barber was, after all, a favourite prison fantasy. But when the chance finally came, I lost my nerve. How would I handle the small talk? The 'innocent' questions?

Professional personal encounters outside can be a nightmare after so long behind bars. Such situations invite fib-telling, to avoid awkward moments and mutual embarrassment. But you tell one small lie, then another, and the hole gets deeper.

Anyway, just when my mirror was beginning to reflect the wild man of Wormwood Scrubs, I found a place. It was late afternoon when I happened to glance through the big window. Inside, a man was sweeping around a row of empty barber's chairs. I took a deep breath and entered. The barber asked me what I'd like. 'Just a trim,' I said. There were no awkward questions, though he sniggered at one point, 'Ah, you cut it yourself?' I squirmed. Should I blame 'the wife'? or 'the sister'? Instead, I confessed. 'Yes,' I replied, adding, 'It was a time thing.' He smiled and said, 'I understand.'

2 October 2003

Blainewatch

Up close, David Blaine is looking positively feral. Through the lens of my telescope, which brings his bearded, sleepy-eyed face to within what seems like touching distance, I note the colour of his skin and the whites of his eyes. Perhaps it's the reflection from the sun-dappled Thames, but a measure of yellowing is definitely apparent. And his hair... unwashed and uncombed for more than four weeks, it's no wonder he's scratching so much, I think.

He surprises me with a wave. Embarrassed at having been

spotted taking such an intrusive nosey into his lair, I lower my optical aid and blush. Then a cacophony of shrieks from a gaggle of schoolgirls nearby signals a more likely target for the wave.

'He's waving at me!' shouts one.

'No! It's me!' yells another.

'He does more waving than the Queen,' says an elegantly dressed woman to my left.

Blaine is back in my sights. Wave, scratch. Thumbs up, scratch. I can't help thinking that he must be stinking in there. For nothing ripens a human more than a spell of bang-up. I know this so well. It is the perfect way to become acquainted with your own multifarious smells. At first, they disgust you. But soon you begin to enjoy them – the comfort they bring, the sense of security they instil.

I wonder if Blaine knows that to make time pass quickly in solitary confinement you must slow down your thinking. This takes discipline. But it enables you to reflect effectively, to examine your life – and your motives. His appear vague. Money certainly, and fame. But I think it's also something deeper; perhaps he has a restless mind, or just a troubled one. If that's the case, a little deprivation, in isolation, can work wonders. I know that too.

A small cloud breaks and beautiful rain falls on my face. It's time to go back to prison, but I walk away smiling. 'Above the Below'? Give me the outside of the inside any day.

7 October 2003

An anxious plan

It seemed like a good idea at the time: a visit to an old friend. It would be a chance to talk about old times, share a few smiles, a few laughs – and catch up on the gossip. I can't remember who mentioned it in a letter first – me, or Big Rinty. But the closer it came to happening the more I wondered whether it was really such a wise move after all.

Ages ago Rinty told me about a visit he had made during his

three years of freedom before he was recalled, to a pal he had left behind after his release. His friend, Mac, still had a few years inside ahead of him and the Big Yin wanted to go and see him to give him some encouragement. They had been in the prison band together, he explained: Mac on bass guitar and Rinty, fair play to him, on lead vocals. 'I waited until I was on my feet,' he said. 'I wanted to show Mac that it could be done. All he had to do was keep going.'

I told Rinty that I didn't think I could do it – go back to prison to visit somebody. It was nothing to do with wanting to forget, either. It was just the idea of going back for a couple of hours and then leaving your pal again, knowing exactly the life that you are leaving him to. 'I would feel as if I was flaunting my freedom,' I said. 'It would be like rubbing his face in it.'

Rinty disagreed. He said that loyalty was more important than giving in to confused personal feelings. 'If you are free and you have got a mate back in there and he's prepared to send you a VO (visiting order), you have to go.'

Well, the fact is I'm not free yet. No matter how much it seems like it sometimes, my day of real liberty is still some months off. And even then it isn't guaranteed. But, then again, nothing is during a sentence like this. In the end I think that was why I decided it was a good idea to try to get to see Rinty while I could. I think I mentioned something about it in one of my letters to him. In one of his he replied, 'I've got plenty of spare VOs if ever you find yourself at a loose end.' When I wrote back I said I would try and get over to see him once I had got myself a car.

Me and my bright ideas. Now I have got the car I have no excuses. I thought, however, that I had better check with one of the governors just to make sure there were no rules barring me from visiting another prisoner while I am still doing time myself – and I wouldn't have been too disappointed if there had been.

I had spent too much time thinking about it. If Rinty had known that it was making me anxious, I know for a fact he would have told me to leave it for a while. References to the visit in his letters were always accompanied with phrases such as 'Only

come if you have got nothing better to do,' or 'Don't worry if
you can't make it.' What a wimp I was being. And the governor
I spoke to thought it was a great idea.

One of the (many) odd things about prison life is that, on the
one hand, if you don't 'mix' on the landings, you are in danger of
being labelled 'anti-social' in staff reports. But if you are released
on parole and you socialize with people you knew in prison then
you are in danger of having your parole revoked for 'mixing with
the wrong sort of people'.

I knew a man doing life who was recalled for this very reason.
He had been in so long the first time that the only people he felt
comfortable with out there were those who had done time too
and understood where he was coming from. Not surprisingly it
took him years to get back out again. So I was pleased with the
governor's response. Really I was.

'As soon as you send me a VO and the details of visiting times,'
I wrote to Rinty in my next letter, 'I'll phone the jail and book
a visit.'

The problem is, I know the pattern of Rinty's day too well. I
know the three times a day his cell door opens and the three
times it closes. I know the times he collects his meals, the times
he eats, the times he sleeps – if he sleeps. It is a routine I broke
away from more than two years ago, but one he is still practising
after twenty-four years.

Anyway, I am committed now. The VO arrived a couple of
days ago. I phoned Rinty's prison the same day and booked a
visit for the weekend. 'Table 22,' said the visits officer. 'Fine,' I
said, 'see you then.'

9 October 2003

A painful visit

Rinty looked well, if a little tense. I had been sitting at our allot-
ted table in his prison's visiting hall for nearly twenty minutes,
watching the door at the far end open and close, letting prison-

ers in one at a time, when finally the big man walked in.

The prison officer supervising the door said something to him and he smiled before turning his head and feigning a nonchalant glance around. When he failed to catch my eye I felt for him instantly. Visits bring prisoners pleasure and pain in equal measure and I understood how vulnerable he would be feeling at that moment; I knew the effort it would be taking to calm his churning stomach and slow his racing mind.

The prison officer handed Rinty a green sash to pull over his navy T-shirt, and then pointed him in my direction. I stood up and he signalled that he had seen me by raising his eyes and nodding. Immediately his face appeared to relax and his smile looked more genuine. When he arrived at our table I reached across and gripped his outstretched hand.

'Good to see you,' I said.

'You too,' he replied.

We sat down and began talking straight away. Two years had passed since we had said our last goodbyes but our conversation was surprisingly easy – almost as if no time had passed at all. I commented on how grey his hair had become.

'Better having grey hair than nay hair,' he retorted.

'Hmm,' I said. Time to go up to the tea hatch.

When I returned he asked me about the journey. I told him it had been great: 160 miles – my first big driving adventure. 'Motorways, trunk roads, dodging speed cameras, Al Stewart tape blaring. Some crazy drivers out there though,' I said.

'Mmm,' he replied.

We had been chatting for just a few minutes when the door leading to the wings opened and a man who I recognized appeared. 'Christ,' I said. 'Raistrick.'

'You know him?' Rinty asked.

I told him that Raistrick had been the first person I had spoken to after one transfer to a Category B jail in 1992. I had walked onto the old Victorian wing, four landings high, dragging six transit boxes full of kit behind me. The cell I had been allocated was on the top landing, but of the dozens of faces peering down from the railings, not a single one showed any interest in helping me. Not that I expected or wanted any help. But then up strolled Raistrick and a couple of his pals. They scooped up the boxes and between us we did the four flights of stairs in one hit.

'It turned out they were the God Squad,' I said. 'But it wouldn't have bothered me anyway. I'd been through the religious phase myself by then and had got a lot from it.'

Rinty snorted. 'He's still going through it,' he said. 'Now he calls himself "the Reverend".' We laughed at that.

Raistrick was moving towards a table close to ours and as he got nearer he noticed me looking at him. I saw recognition spark in his eyes and he came over.

'I'm surprised to see you coming back to one of these places,' he said, offering his hand.

'I'm surprised to see you're still in one,' I replied, shaking it. He obviously thought I was out proper. Rinty shot me a look.

'Twenty-eight years now,' said Raistrick, 'and still going strong, with the Lord's help.'

'Christ,' I said (to which he responded by raising a disapproving eyebrow). 'Well, good luck.'

'Thanks. You too,' he said, before walking over to a table where a large woman sat alone, waiting. Rinty and I looked at each other for a second and then carried on talking.

We covered a lot of ground that afternoon, my pal and I. Rinty told me that the Gambler was doing well in his open jail. 'He's just waiting to be passed for paid outside work,' he said. I told him about Cody's appeal hearing. 'He's due up at the end of this month. This time it's make or break time.' Another couple of refills of our teacups and then our chatting was brought to an unnatural end by a prison officer's booming voice. 'Time's up please, ladies and gents.' I'd forgotten how quickly an hour and a half passes during a visit. Rinty was cool. 'Well, that's it,' he said.

Around the room men, women and children began rising from their seats. Couples embraced, some more passionately than others, and children cried.

'Right,' I said. 'You take it easy in there.'

'Same goes for you out there.' A handshake and an awkward nod later I was walking back to the exit, unable to look back.

16 October 2003

The angry newcomer

Hostile neighbours come with the territory on a prison landing. It's a matter of trust, I suppose. You may get a polite nod or an 'all right mate?' when you first arrive as some try to sound out the level of threat you might pose, or the material worth you might have in your transit boxes. But it can take many weeks for someone new to the system to connect with a circle of acquaintances he feels safe around – many months if there is no one about who knows him and who can vouch for him. It is the nature of the environment, the way of a closed penal community.

One of the good things about being in open conditions is that, generally speaking, prisoners are more open with each other. Not necessary friendly – but not unnecessarily unfriendly. Everybody here remembers how they felt about leaving the closed system – the relief, the euphoria – and no one wants to put the dampers on the expectations of hopeful hearts. But occasionally people land who find the relaxed regime so alien that even without being confronted with any apparent hostility they still feel the need to keep their defences up high. It doesn't happen often, but when it does it normally involves people who have been in a particularly long time – which was why I was puzzled by the defensive behaviour of a neighbour of mine who moved into a room a couple of doors down some weeks ago.

He hadn't been long in the place – two, three months at most – but plenty long enough to have settled down. He was too young to have been in the adult system for more than two or three years, I thought. Unless he'd spent serious time in the YOIs during his sentence, there was no obvious reason why he should be going out of his way to be so antagonistic.

The corridors here are narrow. Whenever people pass, one or

91

the other has to step aside — it's accepted etiquette. Usually both move, both grin bashfully, both mutter a slightly embarrassed 'Thanks,' and on our way we go.

But not my new neighbour. He moved for nobody — simply marched on, shoulders back, eyes (glaring) to the front. Prat, I used to think as I gave way. In some ways he reminded me of Ten Men, a slightly-built youngster I knew years ago in a high-security jail known as Monster Mansion by the local populace. To keep the predators at bay, crop-haired Ten Men walked the landings with his chest inflated to its not very impressive maximum and his arms at an angle that suggested he was carrying two invisible 56lb bags of potatoes. Sadly, his strutting failed to save him. Vulnerable is vulnerable, no matter how you try to disguise it. But that's another story — and this is no Monster Mansion.

I still don't know my new neighbour's name but we at last managed to have a conversation the other night. He'd blanked me so often, ignoring my greetings of 'Mornin'' or 'Evenin'' and my smiles that were intended to disarm. In the end I had to blank him back. I didn't want him to start thinking that I was the weirdo.

We were in the laundry room. Just the two of us. There was silence between us, but it didn't feel awkward — not now my defences were up too. Then he spoke. 'Is that your stuff in the dryer mate?'

His friendliness threw me. 'Yes,' I said, without turning my head.

As I pondered whether to lower my guard and engage him in amicable chat, he spoke again. 'It's all right here. I'm going to miss it if I don't get a result at appeal next week.'

'You're on appeal?' I asked, missing the inference that his place in open conditions was at risk. 'A friend of mine is up on appeal next week,' I said. I was going to tell him about Cody. How he's been waiting nearly twenty-five years for his appeal. But before I could elaborate he interrupted me.

'Oh, it's not me who's appealing. It's the prosecutor. He didn't think I got long enough. He's going to ask the Court of Appeal to increase my sentence. Any more than a year and I'm going back to a closed prison.'

For the next half hour I hardly got a word in. It was clear that he was as anxious as he was hopeful and I even found myself warming to him. But it was getting late and eventually I had to bring our talk to an end. 'Well, good luck,' I said, genuinely wishing him well as I gathered up my stuff.

'Thanks,' he said. 'Thanks a lot.'

Afterwards I thought about how differently you can feel about a person once you know their troubles.

23 October 2003

Lifers

Depicting prison life was clearly not Rex Bloomstein's intention when he made *Lifer: Living with Murder*, shown on Channel 4 on Monday night. In fact it was hard to get more than a flavour from his film of what it is like to spend a day, never mind twenty years or more, as an average prisoner on the landings of a British prison. But since there was nothing average about the prisoners to whom we were introduced, I won't hold that against him.

So what was it about? In 1982 Bloomstein filmed a group of lifers. Monday night's film revisited four of his subjects – Ted, Bob, Steve and Ken – twenty years later. Of the four, three were still in prison. Only Ken was shown being let out – for the third time, for Ken was a 'recall'. Lifers let out on licence can be recalled to prison at any time. They do not have to have committed a further offence. They only need to demonstrate behaviour in the community which 'causes concern' in the eyes of their probation officer. Ken had committed no further offence: his cause for concern was his immoderate use of alcohol. However, bleak as Ken's story was, it was the only one of those featured that inspired any hope for the life-sentence process – and then it was only a glimmer.

As an uncompromising portrayal of stark tragedy, of lives lost and lives wasted, Bloomstein's film was superlative. Harrowing first-hand accounts of horrific events and actions told in deadpan grisly narrative made for gripping viewing. It was documentary television at its most powerful. He managed to bring viewers nauseatingly close to some of the raw, open wounds that abound among the lifer population and, though he only managed to lift a corner of the veil that shrouds their shadowy existence, it was all that was needed.

As a graphic and potent antidote to anyone who still believes that going to prison is no harsher than say, a stay in a holiday camp, we saw that Ted, Bob, Steve and Ken had all aged badly inside. Steve had fared worst of all. From his cell in 1982 he recounted numerous incidents of beatings and enforced sedation (the infamous liquid cosh) that he had been subjected to by mob-handed prison officers. With his athletic build and forth-right way of talking, it wasn't difficult to imagine the violence that must have occurred with each confrontation. We were told that Steve was known to fellow prisoners as the Robin Hood of the system because of his reputation for fighting it. He fought the authorities at every opportunity, smashing up cells 'over a hundred times'. By then he had served twelve years, two of them in Broadmoor, of a minimum twenty-five. When asked if he thought he would survive the full sentence he said, 'I doubt it.'

Twenty years later, Steve's appearance is enough to make the hardest of hearts weep. Now in a secure psychiatric unit and looking and sounding several decades older than his forty-nine years, it is evident that he has been broken, crushed and compre-hensively defeated. Everybody but Steve knows it. He may still be breathing, but he has not survived.

In 1982, Bob told us that there was 'something wrong' with him. He needed 'treatment', he said. He needed to be 'in a hos-pital', he said. His agitation was only just under control, you felt. You did not need to have a diploma in advanced psychiatry to recognize that Bob's argument had merit. Why it took nineteen years before Bob got any effective treatment is a question that will never be satisfactorily answered, if it is ever asked in the first place. He finally found what he craved on the personality-disorder wing of one of the country's most secure prisons. Now sunken-eyed and bloated, Bob seemed happy enough to be getting appropriate attention at last, but I fear his sentence is just beginning.

It's hard to know what to say or think about Ted. We first met him as a dark-quiffed, inarticulate man inhabiting a sparse prison cell with barely any comprehension of the enormity of the offence that had brought him there. Twenty years pass and though the quiff is now a greasy silver, the face gaunt and blanched (except for the black rings around the eyes), there is little evidence of change. Then, through the fog of total institutionalization, Ted at last reveals a sliver of remorse, asking, 'How can I put it right? What I did... how can I put it right?' It is both a heartening and a heartbreaking moment that sadly comes twenty years too late.

Nevertheless, with those few words Ted could have been speaking for all life-sentence prisoners, as well as summing up the meaning of this film for me. It was, I believe, a film about the prison of the mind and the knowledge of terrible deeds done, from which there can never be release.

30 October 2003

It's all over for Cody

Cody's mobile was switched off when I tried to call him last Thursday. His appeal hearing had been in progress since Monday and I had been calling him at the end of each day to see how it was going. The previous evening our contact had been brief. 'It ain't looking too good,' he told me. An important witness had performed badly when giving evidence. 'He looked like he had the hump with everybody,' Cody said.

The witness, a former policeman involved in Cody's initial arrest twenty-five years ago, was unhappy because he had to take time off work to attend court. It was costing him more than the regulation £60 a day expenses allocated by officials and he had decided to voice his gripes in open court. Cody was understanding, to a point. 'I'm sorry it's costing him money,' he said, 'but I'm fighting here to get my life back.'

Up until that phone call I had been confident that Cody's murder conviction and the life sentence that came with it were going to be overturned. All it needed, I believed, was for the anomalies in his original trial – the contradictions, the cover-ups and the instances of blatant abuse of procedure – to be aired in front of a senior judge who could listen to the arguments objectively, with all the relevant information in front of him.

I am no legal expert but I had been troubled after reading Cody's papers a few years ago. I had known about his case for some time – most long-termers got to hear of it eventually.

Long before I met him I knew he was a man who was held in high regard on prison landings up and down the country. I also knew that his case was thought to be 'dodgy' by most who knew him. I am uncertain about how I knew that. Like so much knowledge that seems to drift endlessly around prisons, you are never sure who told you what or if it was just something you overheard. Most of the information you pick up is useless, but you keep your eyes and ears open anyway. Over a period of time a general picture builds in your mind, so that eventually, whether you want to or not, you just know who's who in the prison world.

Cody could be as funny as anyone I have ever met, but he could be serious too when serious was called for. One day he might be entertaining local pensioners invited to a specially organized prison Christmas party (long after he had become a pensioner himself); the next he might be standing his ground against heavy-handed prison officers who had taken a poor view of the fact that he had more than one prison-issue pullover in his possession. More than twenty years inside had not undermined his human qualities. So it was difficult not to like him really.

As for the rightfulness of his conviction – well, that was never something I spent much time thinking about until I read his papers. It didn't affect me personally. Everybody in prison has problems. On the landings a man claiming to be innocent is not that unusual. He just has to get on with it along with everybody else.

The more I got to know him, of course, the more it was impossible not to think occasionally of how appalling it would be if Cody really had been 'fitted up'. Felix the Gambler was convinced. I knew that instinctively. But Felix had known Cody longer than I had. To me, Cody was just a good man to be around in an unpleasant place. We would walk around the exercise yard, me, Cody, the Gambler and Big Rinty. You would never guess we had more than eighty years in prison between us as we strolled, chatting, smiling and sometimes arguing.

Cody used to talk about his family a lot. His two daughters and his son had grown to adulthood while he had been inside. Prison visiting halls were where he was introduced to his new grandchildren as they came along. At the last count there were seven.

After calling and finding his mobile switched off last week I feared the worst. So I tried his home landline and was surprised when he answered.

'How's it going?' I said.

'Well,' he said. 'Up until the last minute I thought I was going back in. There were all these arguments going on. Then the judge lowered his glasses and ordered my release. It was over – twenty-three years in prison for something I didn't do. It was over.'

Not much I can add to that. But there is no happy ending for our friend and his family. Just a less unhappy ending than it could have been.

6 November 2003

The demon sneezer

There are a lot of coughs and sneezes going around the jail at the moment. It is always the same at this time of year. No matter how hard you try to guard against a contagion – with vitamin C supplements, cod-liver oil and hot-water bottles – we live so close to one another that when one person goes down with something, everyone ends up with it eventually.

So far I have been lucky this year. Not spending so much time in the place has helped I suppose. And I do not need to cram myself into the back of the prison van twice a day either, now I have the car. But that only gets me as far as the station. I still have to sit in a packed train carriage for the best part of an hour each weekday morning and evening. I don't mind that, except too often it leaves you exposed to the seasonal bugs of others.

Only a couple of evenings ago I found myself sitting next to a demonic sneezer who had obviously set off for work ill-prepared for a virus manifestation. Without a hanky, tissues, or even toilet paper, the man had nothing but his hands to stop the rest of us from getting showered with his contaminated mucus spray. His sneezes came in threes and with all seats taken and the aisles chock-a-block with upright bodies there was no hiding place.

As a protective measure, each time the sneezer began his build-up, the woman opposite and I held our broadsheet newspapers up high and close to our faces. The man facing our germ-laden travelmate tried his best to do the same with a tabloid freesheet. Haaarghtchoo! Haaarghtchoo! Haaarghtchoo! Three emphatic eruptions. Sympathetic exclamations of 'Bless you' were conspicuous by their absence. I was sure my epiglottis was going to tingle in the morning (usually the first sign of an infection) but so far so good.

In case anybody was wondering, being ill in jail is no fun at all. If you can persuade the prison doctor that you are a genuine case you might get a few days 'sick in cell'. But don't expect hours of uninterrupted recuperative rest. Just as you are nodding off an hour or so after breakfast, the cell door will be flung open and in will march a couple of prison officers on daily 'locks, bolts and bars' duty. They will hammer the window bars with a baton – to make sure you haven't been sawing through them in the night – and 'test' the bolt on the door by rattling it back and forth violently several times. Locks will be tested with five or six robust turns of the key, and maybe a kick or two of the wide-open door thrown in for good measure. You can try to ignore the intrusion by hiding your head under the covers if you like, but it will be difficult with the officers demanding sceptically, 'What's up with you then?'

Once they have gone you will have landing cleaners banging on your door all day asking, 'What are you doing in there?' or, 'Have you got a Rizla?' If you want to eat, when your cell door is opened at lunchtime and again at teatime you will have to get up and join the queue at the servery – or risk an irate servery officer appearing at your doorway with his clipboard to enquire, 'Not eating then?' If you really are poorly, going sick in cell is unlikely to give you much of a respite, though the upside is that once the day is over you could be so exhausted that you can't help but fall into a good night's slumber.

Prison can do strange things to a person. A fellow convict who once occupied a cell near me used to trade most of his prison wages for cheese stolen from the kitchens. Just before bedtime he would eat the cheese in big lumps in order to induce nightmares. Even by prison standards this was odd behaviour. When I eventually asked him why he did this, he said, 'So that when I wake up, being in here doesn't seem so bad.' A fine example of twisted logic.

I am a bit like that when it comes to illnesses. Since being in prison I have not minded the occasional bout of something viral (and prison viruses are famously monstrous). Feeling so wretched that just the flicker of an eyelid fires daggers of pain from the scalp to the toenails is a great way of being reminded how wonderful it is, even in unfavourable circumstances, to normally enjoy good health. So many people don't.

13 November 2003

ERWIN JAMES

Prisoners' Week

Not a lot of people know it, but this is Prisoners' Week. To tell the truth, I didn't know it myself until I overheard a conversation in the showers late the other night between Slabs and Larrson. Slabs, who had recently taken over as the prison van driver, was getting irritated as he laboured to convince the younger man that there really was such a week. The washing machines were out of order and I was scrubbing my socks in the communal sink and trying not to eavesdrop. But as their chat grew louder, and since there was no one else around, it soon became impossible not to take notice. 'I'm telling you,' Slabs exclaimed finally, 'It's true. I heard about it last week on the Wogan show.'

The Wogan show seemed an odd source from which to learn such a pertinent piece of information. How come there was nothing on the house-block noticeboard about it? Or in the gatehouse? No governors had mentioned it as far as I was aware. If it was true you would think somebody in charge might have said something. What was it all about anyway? Was it something we should be celebrating, for example?

As Larrson and I listened, Slabs recounted what he had heard on the van radio as he flitted back and forth to the train station that morning. A priest had been talking on the programme's religious slot. He had visited a prison in the Far East and met men who had been sentenced to spend their natural lives inside. One of the lifers had shown him a tattoo he had had done on his leg, a Bible quote. The priest was so impressed that he had decided to have one done too. It was a great story, and a clever way for him to introduce this forthcoming week for prisoners, however improbable it might sound.

It was then I remembered. It was a religious concept. Some years ago – actually a good fifteen or sixteen, maybe more – I was sitting at the back of a prison chapel when the chaplain announced it was 'Prisoners' Sunday'. He said it marked the beginning of Prisoners' Week, 'a week when thoughts and prayers

100

should be directed towards prisoners and their families...', or words to that effect, blah, blah, blah. I remember squirming with embarrassment. Going to chapel was something relatively new to me then. I had been persuaded by a very kind psychologist who was also a Christian. 'Give it a try,' she had said. 'You have nothing to lose.'

Well, I went, and to my surprise I liked it. My attendance became regular. It was a good place to think. There was no overt sign of conflict, no violence. Prayers and hymn-singing were like communal meditation. The prison chapel, I discovered, was a shelter in a storm, an oasis of peace in a wild and hostile land, the perfect refuge for scoundrels. I didn't mind too much that most of what the chaplain had to say had little or no relevance to my life. And it was good to meet people from the outside community. Some called them the 'do-gooders' (do-gooders mixing with the do-badders), but there was no doubting that most of the outside visitors who attended Sunday service were open-hearted people who believed there was merit in sharing an hour's communion with some of society's fallen.

In the main they were people who would say of prisoners if they were asked, 'There but for the grace of God...' Being in the company of such people helped to bring a sense of balance back into our existence. It gave a modicum of relief from the constant condemnation and intimidation on the wings – from those in authority, and from each other. Meeting people who expressed no desire to judge others had a humanizing effect. The whole chapel thing did – so long as you didn't take it too seriously. But I thought Prisoners' Week was a sentiment too far.

By all means, I remember thinking at the time, express some goodwill towards those in prison if you must. But to promote the idea that prisoners are some sort of needy collective worthy of a special week of 'thoughts and prayers', while at the same time standing by and allowing conditions and attitudes to exist in prisons that evidently damage so many who experience them, was, to my mind, naive at best.

That is probably why I forgot about it until Slabs and Larrson and their argument reminded me – and why I was surprised it was still going, given the scandalous rise in prison numbers since the first time I heard about it, and the lack of any real progress in penal reform.

20 November 2003

Suffering Sheldon is no longer superfit

The illness that laid Sheldon low last year was a mystery. He had only been here a few months when he was struck down. To begin with people thought it was just another bug – a severe bout of the flu, maybe. And nobody really cared, so long as he kept himself at arm's length in the meal queue. Then his condition worsened. To me, it looked like stress.

At well over six feet tall, broad at the shoulder and narrow at the hip, Sheldon had stood out from the crowd. He liked to set the pace in the prison gym. He wasn't the strongest among the regulars, not by a long chalk. But when it came to the iron-man stuff, such as endurance circuit-training and timed sculling on the Concept rower, no one could touch him.

Before starting his workout he would take out his performance logbook, check his times, make a few notes. Eyes would flick in his direction as he sucked in huge chest-inflating breaths, which he would hold for several seconds before blowing out in long, controlled gusts. He'd kick his heels and shake his hands to speed up his circulation before his ten-minute warm-up routine: squat thrusts, burpees, star-jumps, each interspersed with a set of sit-ups.

New arrivals who want to claim a prominent place in the prison hierarchy will often start off in the gym. For, in jail, levels of strength and fitness translate directly, in primitive terms, into capacity to cause harm. The stronger and fitter a man is, the more capable he is perceived to be of causing serious injury in combat. Gym posturing – grunting, glaring, roaring, crashing heavy weights to the floor after massive lifts, everything short of actual chest-beating (though that too is not unknown) – is the safer and less problematic way of letting your neighbours know the score. Word soon gets around.

Sheldon appeared to be posturing a little at first. But it turned out there was nothing sinister about his quest for super-fitness.

Though he always worked out alone, he was never unsociable. After our Saturday morning sessions he would often join me and Tank for our cool-down stroll around the football field. He would talk about his plans. 'I have been lucky from the start,' he told us. 'In every jail I have been in over the past five years I have managed to get the gym orderly's job.' The gym orderly is responsible for keeping the gym clean and generally assisting the PE instructors. It is a plum job with bags of prestige and provides opportunities for almost unlimited gym use. 'It's given me an interest in sports science,' he said. He explained that he had been studying it to degree level. 'My dream now is to open my own gym on the out.' Well, that figured, Tank and I agreed.

So that was Sheldon, certainly one of the fittest men I have ever met in prison. Intelligent, sociable, focused. It did occur to me that if he had fallen ill in any of the closed prisons he had been in, his friends, if he was fortunate enough to have any, might have worried about him. Otherwise his plight would have been ignored. Many of his fellow gym users might even have rejoiced, secretly crowing, as is the way. For everyone in the hierarchy beneath Sheldon would get to move up a place – and the few above him would be able to breathe a little easier. Keeping your place is stressful. But here in open conditions, few get happy when somebody falters or fails. Everybody's planning for a future they can see.

When it became clear that Sheldon was seriously ill there was genuine sympathy. Seeing a man once so fit waste away week after week was frightening. They never discovered the cause, but the good news is that he recovered after a spell in the outside hospital. So much so that when he became eligible for paid work this year he got a job as a fitness instructor at a local gym. I never saw much of him after that, but when I did, every few weeks or so, I would make a point of telling him how well he looked. 'Thanks,' he would say, laughing.

But whatever affected him last year has struck him down again. He is just back from another stay in the outside hospital. When I saw him the other night I almost didn't recognize him, he had lost so much weight. We exchanged a few words, then I left him in his darkened room. It is stress again, I am sure of it. But it is not my place to tell him that I think he is trying too hard for that dream.

27 November 2003

Memories of Officer Bill

No matter what anyone says, being locked in a cell is bad news. It was not something that concerned me greatly early on in my sentence. Prison was a new and peculiar world that had to be learned about and adapted to. Being locked in a cell was the core part of the experience. Everybody inside and outside knew that. The fact that it caused me fear and panic every time my door was banged shut was an irrelevance. It was something that had to be accepted – and quickly.

I had no idea how other prisoners coped with it. My first year was spent on twenty-three-hour bang-up. When the doors were opened briefly for meals to be collected or short walks on the exercise yard, the high-speed conversations revolved around appeal prospects, jobs (crimes) done and future jobs planned. There was lots of gossip – 'He's a grass. He's a nonce' – and some denigrating banter about prison officers. But not once did I hear anyone express distress at being banged up in isolation for so long. So I kept my concerns to myself.

Three or fours years later I was into my stride. Bang-up was a more manageable thirteen or fourteen hours a day. It was still a minor trauma every time the door was slammed shut. But the fear lasted only seconds. I'd soon have my head down reading or studying. Or I'd do my exercises and plan what I was going to listen to on the radio that evening. (There was no television in cells then.)

In fact, I think by that point bang-up had become something I looked forward to at the end of the day. Life on the wing was draining – keeping up a front among fellow prisoners, being under constant scrutiny by prison officers. Isolation brought a certain amount of relief. By morning, however, my heart would pound with the anticipation of the cell door being opened again. The sound of a key turning in the lock seemed to inject new life into my veins.

One lunchtime bang-up period I listened to a radio phone-in about crime and punishment. A prisoner had managed to get through and was struggling to answer the assertive, articulate presenter. When he was asked to explain what it was like to live in a cell there was a pause. 'Well?' said the presenter impatiently. The prisoner faltered, then said eventually, 'It's... It's... It's mental.' I don't think the presenter caught his meaning. But I did and I suspect that any other prisoners listening would have known it too. Fluctuating mental pressure is probably behind a lot of the odd behaviour that occurs on prison landings every day in jails all over the country, much of it caused by long hours spent alone.

Later that day I spoke about the phone-in to a prison officer who worked my landing at the time. His name was Bill and he smoked a pipe. Bill had been a prison officer for twenty-five years. He was laid-back and always courteous to prisoners. Everybody liked him. When I told him about the prisoner and the phone-in, he told me about something that happened to him when he had been on the landings for only a few weeks. 'I was keen,' he said. 'I wanted to make a good impression.'

He said his colleagues kept telling him that he should never trust prisoners. 'They're always trying to get one over on us,' they said. 'Don't give them an inch.' One of his new colleagues came up to him one day and whispered that they had received intelligence that a prisoner on Bill's landing was plotting to escape and had partly cut through his cell window bars. Bill's colleague told him to go to the man's cell and 'discover' the cut bars while the prisoner was absent. 'You'll get bags of brownie points with the governor,' he said. 'I was up for it,' Bill said. 'More fool me.'

As Bill checked the bars with his truncheon, the cell door was shut behind him. 'I just froze when I heard it,' he said. 'Then panic really set in. My heart was hammering. I ran to the door and started hitting it with my stick. Then I started yelling, "Let me out! Let me out!" But nobody came. Then I started crying. I was only in there ten minutes or so, but I'd never been so frightened in my life. When the door was opened, my so-called colleagues were howling with laughter. I felt so stupid. But it taught me never to take locking up people lightly.'

I heard that Bill passed away the other week. He must have been in his early seventies – an exceptional age for a retired prison officer. It was sad news.

4 December 2003

Prison is bad for your mental health

Anne and her colleague Lesley, two mental-health workers, wrote to me recently seeking my views on their plan to introduce a series of self-help booklets for people in prison. I thought it was a great idea. Keeping a balanced view on the world is no easy task inside, especially in the closed system. Living in the midst of frustration, anger, confusion and fear takes its toll. Coupled with so much time spent in that most confined of spaces – the head – it's a wonder that most prisoners manage their imprisonment as well as they do. For prison, as it stands, is not good for your mental health.

The initial process – of arrest, conviction and sentence – is stressful, and then there's the radical change of environment. I wouldn't disagree with anyone who says that people who cause serious harm to others deserve to be imprisoned. And I guess the average man or woman in the street would be disappointed if that did not involve a measure of inconvenience, discomfort and anguish. I'm not convinced, however, that any reasonable person would really want people in prison to suffer significant mental deterioration while inside. But many prisoners do decline. That, I think, is because there is so much more to prison than physical confinement.

My first encounter with the unusual mental effects of prison life occurred years ago in a high-security jail. I had only been there a few months when a man in a nearby cell began acting strangely one morning. We had been neighbours since the day I had landed. He had introduced himself, given me a rundown of the regime and asked if there was anything I needed. It was a working prison and I ended up in the same workshop as my neighbour. We talked daily, until the morning I was washing my food tray in the recess and he walked in and pressed the tap in the next sink.

'Mornin',' I said.

He made no reply. Perhaps he hadn't heard. I turned full on towards him, smiled and raised my voice. 'Mornin'.'

He just stared down at the running water, blanking me. A smack in the face would have been less offensive. In my cell I tried to figure it out. The longer I spent thinking about it, the greater the threat I believed my neighbour posed. In the workshop I avoided him. Sooner or later there would be a confrontation. The only question was when. He had a couple of close associates on the wing. I would have to keep my eye on them too. My options were limited. Should I wait for an ambush? Or should I get my attack in first? Over the next few nights, sleep was fitful. Every time my cell door was unlocked in the days that followed I would step out prepared for combat, adrenaline pumping like rocket fuel. This was my introduction to the cycle of prison paranoia.

This continued for more than a week, until the day my neighbour disappeared. We learned later that he had been sectioned and taken to a secure special hospital. We also learned that prison officers had discovered a 'hit-list' in his cell containing the names of half a dozen prisoners that he believed were plotting against him. I never found out if my name was on it.

Similar episodes occurred over the years. Some I handled better than others. In order to keep a grip on reality, slights, real or imagined, should not be taken personally, I ascertained.

On a prison landing it feels like everything that gives you pain is personal. Yet none of it is. Nobody truly knows anyone. It is a fabricated environment that runs on fabrication – a serious existence that must not be taken too seriously. Knowing when to disengage gave me an advantage, but I couldn't tell you how I learned that. What I came to understand over time was the fragility of the mind. A steel will can face down a prison wall, but only if the mind remains balanced.

During an interview with a probation officer concerning one of my progress reports I raised the issue. 'You know,' I said, 'the way we live out there – I think it is affecting many of us mentally.'

His furrowed brow indicated this was news. 'Oh?'

'It's wearing us down,' I said.

'Are you saying you think you're mentally unwell?' he asked.

It was not what I was saying and I had to backtrack to ensure that not a hint of such a condition appeared in his report. I never raised the subject again with anyone in authority. But it needed to be addressed. I wish Anne and Lesley's project every success.

11 December 2003

Abuses at Wormwood Scrubs

Before reading the Guardian expose on HMP Wormwood Scrubs last week I was prepared to believe that the former flagship of Her Majesty's Prison Service really had mended its ugly ways. Now I'm not so sure. (The *Guardian* story, based on court documents arising from previous and current attempts by forty-five prisoners to sue the Prison Service for a range of assaults and abuses while serving their sentences over a ten-year period from the early nineties, revealed that the Service settled more than thirty cases out of court and was forced to pay a total of £1.7 million in compensation. In fourteen of the cases the Prison

Service 'submitted to judgment.' This amounted to an admission that it had no defence against the claims brought and would not contest numerous allegations of beatings, mock executions, death threats and other abuses by staff.)

The police investigation into the prisoners' allegations against prison officers took place in the late 1990s. It was widely publicized and resulted in the conviction and jailing of three prison officers.

The investigation caused a lot of anger on the landings at the time. On the outside, good people also voiced their concern. Then it all died down and before long was as good as forgotten. The affair hadn't affected me personally, nor did I know the prisoners involved. There was no reason for me to dwell on those sorry events. Like everyone else in prison, I had my own difficulties to overcome and that was where I focused my energies. Had I realized the extent of the abuses, I doubt that I would have forgotten so easily.

It seems pertinent to me now that the first allegation of serious assaults was made at the Scrubs early in 1994, at the height of the 'Prison Works' campaign (battle cry: 'If you can't do the time don't do the crime'). The vindictive rhetoric reverberated behind prison walls, I recall. For those of us who had been in a while, the sense of disillusionment was almost overwhelming as we felt ourselves becoming even more detached from those on the outside. Efforts made to get back out there and function properly seemed wasted. The popular press was reporting regularly that people in prison had been having too good a time of it for long enough. To bring us back into line, prison life needed to be more rigorous. Regimes should be austere, it was famously, if disingenuously, argued – an argument gleefully received in many quarters – ensuring that public opinion grew more retributive than ever. In all probability the situation would not have come about if the world of prison had not been such an alien place in the minds of the public at large.

Through it all, the most worrying development was the change in the attitude of prison staff. Prison officers who had been generally helpful and respectful hardened up. Seeing the older hands grow ill at ease when discovered by newer recruits to be passing the time of day with a prisoner, or, worse, trying to help by sorting out a phone call or chasing up a missing letter, was disturbing. Prison became a darker place still, making it a lot easier for unscrupulous key men to abuse their positions.

As far as we know, only a minority went the extra mile. But how. The prison service now accepts that over a five-year period there were fourteen cases of brutality by prison officers at HMP Wormwood Scrubs – brutality that included beatings, mock executions and death threats. These uniformed public servants went mob-handed into prison cells and disgraced themselves wholesale. In one incident, up to eight prison officers, including an SO (senior officer: a rank that can take years to achieve), took part in an attack on a lone prisoner. More than once, groups of prison officers made hanging cords from sheets and threatened lone prisoners with the noose while everyone else was banged up. Just think about that for a moment.

At least on the landings you can take your chances among your fellow prisoners. Once behind your cell door it's a different story. If you can handle it you should be safe. But, as events at the Scrubs proved, you are potentially at your most vulnerable. Most worrying for me is the culture of complacency that appears to have existed among senior management. It seems that nobody was bothering to guard the guards. Anyone who goes to prison should expect a major change in lifestyle. Nobody, but nobody, should expect to be intimidated, threatened or tortured by prison staff.

Apparently the Scrubs has been reformed. That is what some people say, anyway. But I think both the outside community and the inside community have a right to know for sure. If society genuinely wants prison to work, lessons need to be learned. The mass ignorance about life in our prisons is a major obstacle to progress. A public inquiry into the outrages at Wormwood Scrubs would help to eradicate the complacency that allows prisoner-abuse to go unchecked.

18 December 2003

A Happy New Year for Felton

Long-term convicts love to reminisce. Talking about prisons we've been in and fellow cons we've known makes up a big part of our exercise yard conversations. Not that I've spent much time on prison exercise yards lately. I'm out and about on the other side of the fence so often these days that I barely have the time or the inclination to stroll around indulging in sentimental jail talk. I still go walking in the grounds when I'm in, but I haven't had a good talk with anybody in here since the Celtic Poet was released in the summer.

I was thinking about this at the weekend and feeling a little lonely as I took a post-festive-season walk around the football pitch when Felton Leaky sidled up beside me. We had last spoken two months earlier when he told me he was waiting for his parole review answer.

'How's it going?' he said. 'Had a good 'un?' Meaning had I had a good Christmas and New Year.

'Yeah,' I said. 'Not bad. Glad it's all over though. What about you?'

Our previous conversations had always been brief but Felton was pleasant enough when we did pass the time of day. Sometimes he would tell me about the progress he was making. Not because we were pals, but because we had done similar amounts of time to get to where we are now, I guess. This territory is unknown to so many. Those of us who inhabit it have a need to share the experience, even if only occasionally, with someone else who can understand.

And Felton is so laid back. Not what you would expect if you knew of his reputation. Eight or nine years ago he was classified as one of the three most difficult control problems in the whole of the prison system. To see him now, with his good job at a local transport company and his little car in the prison car park, you would hardly credit it.

But it hasn't come easy. His stance against the authorities has caused him to spend more years in prison than was strictly necessary. He was four years over his official tariff when he landed here. Thankfully, the people in charge had the confidence to accept that his positive response to open conditions was genuine. They were so impressed with Felton's attitude that they brought his dates forward. In no time he was out doing community work, which brought him into contact with the company that offered him the paid job he's got now. His bosses think a lot of him, apparently.

As we crunched over the frosted grass, exhaling grey clouds of warm vapour with every breath, I braced myself for a conversation with Felton about 'the good old days'. Instead, he beamed at me. 'That was the best Christmas I've ever had in prison,' he said.

'How come?' I asked.

'Because it was my last,' he said. 'I'm out at the end of this month.'

This revelation changed the mood instantly. I slapped his back and within minutes we were laughing and joking like two old compadres. Inevitably we drifted into the past and a comparison with our first Christmases inside.

'I was on remand,' I said, 'Band Aid was number one.'

Felton sniggered.

'Oi,' I said, 'you can laugh. You must have been in then too.'

'I was. I'd just been weighed off [convicted and sentenced]. I landed in reception at Wanno [Wandsworth] and ended up in front of the most miserable-faced screw.'

He then recounted the exchange that followed between him and the sour-faced reception officer. 'After telling me it was his jail and if I fucked about I'd regret it, he started asking me for my stuff, announcing it item by item to his mate who recorded it on a property card. Finally, I'm bollock-naked in front of him except for my bracelet. So he points to it and says, "What's that?"

'"It's me lucky amulet," I said.

'Then he says, "What did you get at court?"

'I said, "Life with a fifteen rec."

'"Well," he says, "it wasn't that lucky was it?" Then he turns to his mate and he says, "One unlucky amulet."'

The empty field echoed with our laughter and then it was teatime and our walk was at an end. Before parting to collect our dinner plates I turned to Felton and said, 'If I don't see you in the next couple of weeks, good luck for on the out.'

'Thanks,' he said, 'good luck to you.'

I took my meal back to my room and ate slowly. Felton's news brought it home to me that I'm also looking at release this year.

8 January 2004

Release plan

Five years ago, almost to the day, I sat in front of a prison officer (whom I will call Mr Fairman) and listened as he explained that now that I was a Category C prisoner I would have to start formulating a 'release plan'. I had landed in his prison in the first few days of the new year after more than fourteen years in high-security conditions. My euphoria at having made the first major downgrade in security classification had quickly dissipated after discovering the limitations of the Category C regime.

Staff shortages and disputes meant bang-up – and plenty of it. Because of an escape some weeks earlier, movement between wings when cell doors were opened was severely restricted. The sports fields were out of bounds, and the exercise area, where we could walk for half an hour a day – if it wasn't raining – had been reduced to little more than the size of a tennis court. It struggled to accommodate the strolling needs of six hundred men. Luckily for those in charge, it was only ever used by sixty or seventy prisoners at a time. But with such dire levels of negativity and lethargy in the jail, I was going to have to dig deep if my stay there was to be worthwhile.

'You've made progress getting here,' Fairman said. 'Now you've got to start thinking about...' He paused and pointed out of the office window, over the razor-wire-topped and steel-clad fences, '...out there.'

It would have been easy to get into a dispute about the definition of 'progress'. His so obviously differed from mine. But I could hardly blame him if he was unable to appreciate my view. Earlier in our talk he had told me that before joining the prison service he had been a milkman, with his own round. Overheads and increasingly stifling regulations made it necessary for him to seek out security for his family elsewhere. 'I had a mortgage to pay and school uniforms to buy,' he had explained. Getting by was his main purpose in life. His hopes and dreams – and his fears – were demanding but manageable to a committed individual.

As I listened he reminded me of how good it could be just to be an ordinary, decent human being. His was the kind of life I had hankered after before coming to prison, but I had never discovered the means by which it could be achieved.

One thing Fairman did understand about my situation, however, was that my journey was far from over. 'The end is still a way off,' he said as our talk proceeded, 'but it's going to come.' He pointed at the floor. 'And here is where you've got to start thinking about it.'

I supposed he had been saying similar things long before I came along. I had been allocated him as my 'personal officer' – an odd prison title that meant he was my first point of official contact for information, guidance and, if requested, assistance. I had been told he had all the lifers. Knowing the system, his superiors would have recognized in his demeanour a natural ability to encourage calm in troubled souls. Somebody who could settle long-termers, many of whom would have served ten or more long stretches of solid time behind high walls, would be a valuable asset to prison managers. Not that I thought there was anything phoney about Fairman. Despite encounters with so many prisoners serving sentences for the most serious crimes, he appeared not to share the cynicism of many of his more senior colleagues. I liked him for that.

In fact, by the end of our talk I felt that perhaps he did, after all, possess more than a little understanding of what it might be like to walk in the shoes of somebody serving my kind of sentence. Maybe he had learned it from our eyes, our faces, our body language. It was enough for this gentle-mannered man not to allow his work to undermine his good nature – no matter how rigorously he might have been tested. Fair play to him, I remember thinking as he walked me back to my cell. Behind my door, I put all thoughts of 'release plans' and 'getting out' right out of my head, however. The path immediately ahead was still too long and uncertain. I stayed in head-down and keep-focused mode.

It feels different now. A governor told me this week that all parole reports following a series of pre-Christmas call-ups I had had with prison staff had recommended my release. While I am not exactly feeling 'gate happy' yet, the future is more certain than it has ever been before. The parole board sits to consider my case next month. Some weeks after that I will receive an answer. In the meantime I will try not to think about it.

15 January 2004

Cody's new crisis

I am finding it harder and harder to feel good about Cody's success at the Court of Appeal last October. To say I was pleased for him when he was cleared would be an understatement. Everybody who knew him was overjoyed. It was not just the fact that he had survived twenty-three years of wrongful imprisonment either. It was the way he did it – with generosity of spirit, unfailing resilience, and eternal optimism.

To suffer prison conditions for more than a couple of decades and come out smiling is one thing. But along the way, Cody gave encouragement and hope to so many others. At times, people wondered whether his case would get to the appeal-court judges at all. Now that he has been exonerated it is impossible to look at what he endured and not be astounded. I'm not embarrassed to describe the way he handled his predicament as heroic.

Cody's family are heroes, too, in my view. His marriage failed during the early years of his sentence, but friends brought his children on visits. When they were old enough to decide for themselves, his son and daughters chose to stand by him. No matter to which part of the country he was sent to serve what was, in fact, someone else's time – and there were many transfers – their loyalty was unfaltering. When they were struggling to bring up their own children they never missed an opportunity to visit their dad, proudly introducing him to new additions as they came along.

I felt for them most when Cody fell seriously ill in his last closed prison. Rinty, Felix the Gambler and I knew there was something wrong. His face went so grey, and our exercise-yard strolls had been reduced to ambles to accommodate our elderly pal. At the prison healthcare centre, he had been fobbed off many times with aspirin and the like. It was galling, but we thought that in time he would get over whatever it was. Better to give the prison doctor a wide berth anyway, we believed.

His eldest daughter thought differently. She had been so concerned after one visit that, as soon as she was outside the prison gates, she telephoned the emergency services and asked for an ambulance to be sent to the jail to collect her father urgently. When the ambulance arrived, bemused gate staff turned it away. It was a hoax call, a gate officer said. 'Don't worry. If anyone in here needs an ambulance, we'll call you.' Less than a week later he had to make that call when Cody collapsed. His family was later told by the consultant that the odds of Cody making it through surgery had been fifty–fifty.

Everything this man went through would have been bad enough had he been guilty. It looks even more horrific now that we know he was innocent all along. It was this realization of the enormity of what had befallen Cody that tempered my initial surge of joy when I heard of his acquittal. Over the telephone that evening he gave me a rundown of the day's court proceedings. As I listened I felt a profound sense of anti-climax, which I kept firmly to myself.

Afterwards, I thought that would be it for Cody. He had achieved what he had been fighting for all those years. There was compensation to consider, but I surmised that this would be dealt with by lawyers. He had told us many times on the yards and landings that he would fight for financial compensation when it was all over so that he could 'look after the kids'. I guessed that that would occupy his time now.

If I am honest, once Cody had been cleared I did not feel as motivated to keep in touch with him. As I understood it, he had his family and a circle of friends. I believed he was where he wanted to be. I would never have consciously decided to cut off our contact, but I did think that our association would now probably reach its end naturally. I have my own uncontested jail term to concentrate on, after all. Then, during the couple of times we spoke on the phone in the following weeks, I detected his disillusionment. And he said some worrying things. 'There's some bits of prison I really miss sometimes,' he told me once. 'In a way,' he added, 'some of the people I met became like family.'

My efforts to keep in touch were pretty dismal. Christmas came and went and neither of us made contact. I was fine about that, until I found out last week that the reason for his silence was that he was in hospital. This time it is his heart. A bypass operation is scheduled for this week. As soon as he's out of intensive care I'll be straight over to see him.

22 January 2004

Job interview success

The interview went well, I thought. I'd been nervous beforehand, but not unduly so. My preparation had been thorough. CV, references, good ideas in head (to demonstrate initiative and strategic planning ability). And I was confident. If I didn't believe in my heart of hearts that I could manage it – and manage it well – I would never have applied for the job.

I've been thinking about future employment prospects for a while now. With the real possibility of release on the horizon at last, I've needed to be on the look-out for something more substantial than where I am at present. Without question I've loved my work for the small charity that helped me in the past. I'm not sure which has contributed more to my sense of self-worth since I've been in the office: the trust of colleagues, or the responsibility of the post, but both have enabled me to experience job satisfaction like I've never experienced it in my life before.

When I began as a volunteer I'd planned to stay only until I was eligible to enter the job market proper. The charity understood this. But my speed and competence had improved so much that, eventually, paying me for my work appeared to be a logical step. There were advantages for the organization: volunteers are only temporary, whereas I'd be available on the days required for the foreseeable future; and while volunteers often leave just at the point when their familiarity with the office systems and information-sourcing skills have reached their optimum level, my usefulness would have a longer life.

I didn't get my hopes up too high, though. I knew it would depend on whether Nadia, the group coordinator, could raise the funding to cover the post. She had a few knock-backs, but persisted and finally succeeded, turning me instantly from a reluctant state dependant to a happy tax-payer. If it had been full-time it would have been the perfect job.

But I was content. That little job gave me my first real income in nearly twenty years. It gave me self-respect and an opportunity to engage meaningfully with the outside world. I knew I'd be sorry to leave it. I just hoped that I'd be able to move on to something equally satisfying when the time came. I'd barely given it much deep thought, however, when out of the blue Nadia announced she was leaving. 'It's a family thing,' she explained. 'We're moving to the other side of the country.'

This was sad news for the organization. Nadia kept us cohesive and motivated. Her energy was boundless. In her spare time she marched for various causes, standing against anyone or anything that sought to oppress others. Yet her principles did not diminish her sense of humour. We were going to miss her throaty laughter as much as everything else she contributed.

Filling her position was harder than had been anticipated. Even when the thirty or so applicants for her job had been trimmed to a shortlist of four, none proved ideal. Another ad had to be placed. Then Nadia suggested I apply for the job. 'You could do it,' she said. 'I know you could.'

It was kind of her to say so, but the job is a serious one – with huge responsibility. It needs experienced professional skills and qualifications. 'Thanks,' I said, 'but I doubt I could do what you do.'

I was flattered that she thought I could. So much so that I slept on it over a couple of nights and then spoke to a senior member of staff. I needed to know if it was feasible for me to apply. 'Yes,' they said. I made the shortlist. Hence the interview.

I confess, my weaknesses were glaringly obvious: serving prisoner, no professional experience. On the plus side I had enthusiasm and transferable skills learned in jail. Two members of the management committee and one senior member of staff made up the interview panel. They all took notes. One gave me marks out of five for my answers.

'So,' said the elderly gent in the middle, 'do you have any financial management experience?' He'd bowled me a googly. My brain cells searched for an answer. Then it came. 'Well,' I said, 'in nearly twenty years of imprisonment on an average wage of £4 a week, I've never been in debt.' I think that got a three – only someone who'd been in prison would know it was worth a five.

Anyway I must have given some impressive answers. I was called back to the interview room later. It was good news. 'You came second,' said our senior staff member. First choice was the Oxbridge graduate with a proven track record. A job offer has been made. We're waiting to see if it's taken up.

29 January 2004

Mobile phone brings good news

Just occasionally the progress made by civilization while I've been in prison amazes me. But only very occasionally. I'm getting to grips with mobile phones. I have an old one, donated by the Kid when he got out of here the year before last. We are not permitted to have them this side of the fence. They have to be registered and kept at the gate. If you get permission to have one you collect it on the way out and hand it in on your return. Pay-as-you-go only. No credit allowed.

And I've mastered cash machines. How could I ever forget the helpful prison officer in my last closed prison, who just in case it hadn't occurred to me, took it upon himself to explain that things had 'changed out there' during my years of incarceration. 'For example, look at this,' he said, before retrieving a shiny disc from the small plastic purse he had produced from a trouser pocket. 'That's a £2 coin.' It was hard to feign wonder. But somehow I managed.

'Wow,' I said. 'How much is that worth?'

'Oh,' he said sympathetically, 'two pounds.'

Bless.

But novel and comment-worthy as mobile phones and cash machines (and £2 coins) are, I'm not sure they represent particularly significant leaps forward for humankind. The truth is that for all the sense of newness I've experienced since getting my gate pass nineteen months ago – and it really does all feel brand new – I don't think the world has changed that much since I've been away. The Internet is impressive, I admit. And the range of sophisticated electronic gadgetry available is mind-boggling. But I'm loath to accept that such technological changes have brought about greater contentment. At least I was, until my mobile phone rang unexpectedly this week (nothing fancy, just brr-brr, brr-brr) and I heard an unfamiliar voice on the other end addressing me in a familiar manner. 'All right, mate?' it said.

'Er, who is this please?' I asked.

A chuckle followed and then the voice said, 'It's me – Cody.'

Cody? Of course it was him. How come I hadn't twigged? 'Christ,' I said. 'You sound different.'

'Do I?' he said.

'You sound so... so...' I couldn't quite put my finger on it. 'So well,' I said eventually. That was it. He sounded fantastically well, like I had never heard him sound before. When I asked where he was I got an even bigger surprise.

'I'm at home,' he said, 'cooking a pot of rabbit stew.'

All week I had been wondering how he was getting on at the hospital. I had telephoned a couple of times to find out, but since I wasn't a close relative no information was forthcoming. He had told me a little about the operation. He was to have a vein taken out of his leg and attached somehow to his heart to ease the load on the malfunctioning organ. To me that sounded serious. I imagined chest clamps and poking about among exposed, pulsing vitals.

'I told the surgeon not to worry if anything went wrong,' Cody had told me on the phone a couple of days before the op. 'I said, "You can only do your best, doc."'

Typical Cody. Grateful that he was being taken care of properly at last and not wanting the good people who were making efforts on his behalf to feel bad if he didn't make it. He clearly thought it was serious too.

I expected him to ring me when he was out of intensive care and back on a ward recuperating. The hospital he was in is only half an hour or so from my office. My plan was to get round to see him one evening after work. I thought he would be stretched out, with wires and tubes hanging out of his frail frame. I would sit quietly next to him, I thought, perhaps whispering gently about the old times above his laboured breathing. That always seems to help in the films. This new development threw me.

'I've had the op,' he said. 'I was only in the intensive aftercare ward for a couple of days. When I came to I felt 100 per cent. No more pains in me chest. I told the doctor, "It's a miracle." But he said what I've 'ad is routine now. "Well," I said, "it's come to

121

something if miracles like this have become routine.'"

It seems our friend could have another ten or maybe twenty good years ahead of him. Extra time to enjoy a better quality of life; extra time to give the authorities grief for what they did to him; and extra time to spend with his family. Now that's what I call progress.

5 February 2004

Ready for a lucky break

One of the many major defects in my life before prison was an over-reliance on luck. My predominant hope was always that 'something good will turn up'. Sometimes it did, but more often it did not. Even when it did, I was too ill-prepared to take advantage of any positive opportunity that presented itself by chance. 'Good times' were never as good or as long-lasting as they might have been – and bad times only ever got worse.

Figuring out why things were the way they were seemed impossible. Looking back, I can see that much of my perceived 'misfortune' occurred as a result of my poor choice-making. Decisions made after little or no thought about the consequences were invariably bad ones. As a complex life became more complicated, I wondered if I would ever achieve the order I craved. With hindsight, I know that it would have taken a lottery winner's share of luck for that to happen. I hoped and waited, but it never came. Life in prison brought an end to my reliance on luck.

That does not mean I stopped believing in it. Not at all. I have just become better equipped to benefit from it if it happens. The other week, Nadia, the former group coordinator in the office where I have worked for more than a year as an information gatherer, wished me luck before I went in for an interview for her old job. I smiled and said, 'Thanks.' I knew she was rooting for me. She had even promised to provide guidance over the telephone if my application was successful.

'What you lack in experience you'll more than make up for in determination and enthusiasm,' she had said. I valued her faith in me hugely, but the last thing I intended to depend on was luck.

Of the thirty applicants, four, including me, made the shortlist. I had spent long nights filling in the application form and writing up my CV. I had anticipated the kind of questions I might be asked and rehearsed what I thought would be good answers. I thought of a couple of pertinent things to ask the panel, to show I had a heartfelt interest in the organization. I printed several copies of my proposed 'action plan'. It was important to demonstrate, I felt, that I had considered carefully what I could bring to the post.

On the morning, my suit and highly polished shoes completed my preparations. I could have done little more. The fact that I came second out of the four hopefuls had nothing to do with luck.

With impeccable professional standards and a track record to match, the Oxbridge graduate was far and away the best candidate. To come second behind such a high achiever was a notable accomplishment, I believed. The interview had been an excellent experience. None of my research and planning had been wasted. Once the new person settled in, perhaps I would be able to share some of my ideas. But days passed and no response to the job offer was forthcoming.

Telephone calls were made, emails sent. 'I'm still thinking about it,' said the candidate – eventually. 'Let's be patient,' I said during a short staff briefing. The longer we had to wait meant acceptance was more likely. That was my view anyway, ever the optimist.

It was early evening on the tenth day when we were finally informed. Phoebe, our senior member of staff, and I were the only two in the office. I was about to leave when Phoebe said, 'Oh – an email from the candidate.' I looked up and waited for the message to be shared. The uncertainty was over. Then I noted Phoebe's tone of disappointment. 'The offer has been refused.' For the sake of the organization, I was disappointed too.

There was an explanation: something about the parameters of the post being 'insufficiently defined'. Whoever took the post would have to be flexible and a multi-tasker for sure. The demands would be intense and numerous. A high-flying, forward thinker would have welcomed such a challenge, I would have thought.

'So what happens now?' I asked.

'It falls to you.'

'Are you sure?' I said.

'I'm certain. You came second on merit. I'm excited for you. If you want the job it's yours.'

When I called Nadia, she did not need to say she was thrilled. Her howls of joy spoke volumes. Now I am in post and embracing the opportunity. My colleagues are in full support. It may sound contradictory, but sometimes I feel like the luckiest man on the planet.

12 February 2004

The secret graveyard

Buried in the grounds of a small East Midlands prison I was in for much of the nineties are thought to be the remains of some of the prisoners hanged there during the years before the abolition of capital punishment. There is no hard evidence – no gravestones or official notices bearing names or dates. But, during the years I spent there, I heard enough anecdotal evidence to convince me that it was true. The most compelling testimony came from Sister Jean, an elderly woman who had worked as an unpaid assistant to the chaplain for more than thirty years and knew all there was to know about the place.

I had been in the jail just a couple of years when I was given a job keeping the yards tidy. One February afternoon I was sweeping near the steps of the chapel when Sister Jean stopped to chat. After exchanging pleasantries for a few minutes, I decided to ask her if there was any truth in the rumours. She told me without hesitation.

'They're buried over there where the old outside wall used to be,' she said, pointing to a secluded corner six feet or so within the new perimeter wall. 'Opposite the topping shed.'

The topping shed. There was nothing mythical about the small stone former death house, accessed through a tunnel-shaped annexe a short walk from the main prison wing. Since being decommissioned as a place of execution, the shed had been used as a store for 'victuals'. When the outside doors were opened for deliveries you could see high up inside. Two robust parallel cross beams stood out from the rest, for no apparent purpose – until you were told. Then it was obvious.

The bulky construction of the beams ensured that they could regularly withstand the sudden jerking weight of a hanged man as he fell through the trap on the platform below. The trap had long since gone, but the platform remained and served admirably as a sturdy shelf for sacks of oats, flour and other assorted provisions with which to sustain human life – a typical barb of prison irony.

Once I had learned about the secret burial ground, I used to take extra care to keep it neat. There was little to see, just a couple of rows of flowerbeds that had been defeated by the wind, and some shrub borders divided by rarely used earth paths. But it was a beautiful place to spend time thinking and getting my own situation into perspective. However demanding life in prison was, at least I was alive and could still dream about a future.

The funny thing about 'the future' when you are serving a life sentence is that you are less sure than most people that it will ever become a reality. You attend review boards where targets are set and checked at the end of a two- or three-year knock-back.

The official perception of your 'progress' is set down in reports, and for a while it feels as if you have moved forward. You know the time is passing by the changing of the dates and the seasons, and by the coming and going of fellow prisoners. Then, one day, you take a look around and suddenly it feels like you are still in the exact same place. You thought you were ahead, but all you were doing was treading water, expending all your energy in an effort to stay from going under. But it isn't enough to just survive. You have to survive and then some, if you are ever going to be of any use when the time for release finally arrives.

When Sister Jean told me about the people buried in the prison grounds, I felt more determined than ever. The occasional echo of children's laughter from the other side of the wall when I was over in the corner added to the air of poignancy that seemed to hang about the place. After a stint clearing the litter from the unacknowledged graveyard, a bit of bang-up and the organized chaos on the landings never seemed so bad.

Memories of those prison yards and the secrets they hold have been a motivating factor in the way I have served my time for almost ten years now. Any moments of disillusionment or times when I could feel myself flagging have been quickly dealt with by a swift recollection of the topping shed conversation with Sister Jean. There is so much about prison that I do not want to remember when the time comes for me to leave. But not the windbeaten flower beds. Those I never want to forget.

19 February 2004

Felton's cheeky request

From the point of view of the prison system, Felton Leaky's reputation as a 'control problem' was well deserved. It was spawned years ago during his first spell in a segregation unit. During a routine search of his cell, prison officers found a damaged library book and placed him 'on report'. In front of the governor during the subsequent adjudication, Felton explained that the book had been in the cell and damaged when he had moved in. 'You can check,' he told the governor confidently. 'I've only been in your jail a week and not had a chance yet to use the library.'

But (ahem) in those days, prison adjudications were notoriously unjust proceedings. The mere fact that a prisoner had been placed on report was sufficient proof of guilt as far as many adjudicating governors were concerned. And so it was this time. 'Case proved,' said the governor. 'Seven days all round.'

It meant that Felton got seven days' loss of prison earnings, seven days' loss of privileges and seven days in the segregation block. If he hadn't been a lifer he would probably have only lost a couple of days' remission, which he could have claimed back after six months as long as he had no further adjudications in the meantime. Lifers have no remission to lose and so governors are more likely to supplement any punishment with a few 'extras'. If Felton was telling the truth – and a couple of weeks ago, during our last walk around the football pitch, he was still adamant that he had been – then I guess he was entitled to feel aggrieved.

Injustice cuts deep in prison. Felton accepted his life sentence for the crime he committed, but he was not prepared to accept extra, undeserved, punishment from the prison system. Not without retaliation. To get his own back, while in the seg, he saved up a week's worth of his bodily waste in his plastic toilet pot. (This was long before 'slopping out' was all but abolished.) Felton told me that it was the tradition in that jail for men in the seg to be visited by the governor on the morning they were due to go back to 'normal location'. The governor, flanked by two officers, liked to give the seg prisoners a little lecture about the importance of discipline before authorizing their move back on to the landings.

But when Felton's door was opened that morning, a lesson in prison indiscipline was waiting. 'When they saw the pot in my hand they just froze like rabbits caught in headlights,' Felton said. 'I shouted at the governor, "You've just given me a week of shit for nothing. Well, now you can have some back." And then I launched the contents of the pot over the three of them. You should have seen them pulling and shoving each other as they tried to scarper.'

It cost Felton a ship-out and the next three months in various segregation blocks, as well as the first entry of 'control problem' in his prison file. It followed him wherever he went. Staff at receiving prisons were always wary of him and often gave him grief from the off. I think that over the following years he came to see himself as a serial victim of system injustice. Whenever he felt antagonized by prison staff, he responded with the 'shitting up' routine, culminating in the infamous 'vacuum flask refill shit-bomb incident'. The legend was born.

Arguably Felton brought many of his troubles on himself. He certainly did some hard time – and served more than four years over his minimum. But with no incidents for the past five or six years, he at last arrived here. Open conditions, a job, a car. The next step was release. But the other week Felton had one final surprise in store for the governor who came to tell him his parole application had been successful.

'You're out next Tuesday,' said the governor, who was puzzled when Felton's face failed to register gratitude or joy. 'You don't look too happy about it,' he added.

'It's not convenient for me to be released on Tuesday,' said Felton. 'I'm doing an extra shift for a workmate. Can it wait till Friday?'

'What?' said the governor.

'Friday,' said Felton. 'I don't want to be released until Friday.'

Once the governor had stopped laughing, he agreed. Friday came and Felton walked. After nineteen years it was over. He had managed to go on his own terms. A control problem to the end.

26 February 2004

Memories of Sid Fearlittle

Until he landed here last week I hadn't seen Ron Schofield in more than eleven years. Then he had been ahead of me in his life sentence by four or five years. By rights he should have been out long before me. Hiccups along the way, I supposed. Ron and I had never been pals, but once we had recognized each other last Saturday I felt obliged to say hello and give him a rundown about what to expect from this place.

The only trouble was that Ron just wanted to talk about 'the old days' – days that for me are fast becoming another country. Anyway, I went along with the banter for a while until he started slagging off Sid Fearlittle, another con we knew from yesteryear who had saved a prison officer's life in the early nineties.

'Hang on a minute, Ron,' I said, 'you're out of order.'

'Bollocks,' he said – and for the rest of the weekend we blanked each other.

I still think Ron was out of order. Before that incident Sid had always been 'staunch'. What happened was that after a set-to with a governor, Sid had been shipped out of a high-security jail and, because of lack of space in the seg unit, straight into the hospital wing of another. A week later, fire broke out in the hospital's mattress storeroom and the prisoners had to be evacuated.

As the thick, acrid smoke from the smouldering mattress foam seeped into the corridors, visibility fell to zero. Sid was walking blind down a stairwell with his head down and his prison-issue sweater pulled up over his mouth when he saw what he thought was an upturned foot in the doorway of the observation room at the bottom. He tried calling to the prison officer whose voice they were all supposed to be homing in on.

'Just keep coming until you can see me, lad,' the officer called back.

'But guv, there's some poor geezer on the deck in the obbo.'

'Shut it,' called the officer. 'Just get your arse down this end quick where I can see you.'

'Fuck that,' said Sid, and retreated into the fog. Back at the doorway, the foot had disappeared. Sid hesitated, wondering if he had made a mistake, and then felt his way into the room.

'Fearlittle!' shouted the officer in charge of mustering.

With lungs burning and eyes streaming, Sid dropped to his hands and knees and began crawling around the floor, jumper over his mouth. 'Where are you?' he called into the smoke. He was about to give up when his free hand caught against a trousered leg.

The smoke was so thick that he couldn't even make out the rest of the body. Dropping his sweater from his mouth he found the other leg and grabbed a tight hold.

'Fearlittle!'

'He's one of yours, guv,' Sid shouted back, as he dragged the

ERWIN JAMES

inert prison officer along the floor of the hospital corridor.

The man whose life Sid had saved was prison officer Morris, who had been in the service for twenty-eight years and was due to retire a month after the hospital fire. He was so grateful to Sid for saving his life that when he had recovered, he wrote to the parole board on Sid's behalf. Sid ended up with a Queen's Pardon, which translated into thirty days off his eleven-year sentence – not a lot, considering the risk he had taken. But at least Morris managed to get him transferred to a cushier jail where he could enjoy more contact with his family.

Sid lost all his jail cred for saving Morris. Everybody says they would do this or that in an emergency, but who knows until one happens? A lot of cons would have ignored that upturned boot. Most of those who might have taken a look would have backed right off when they discovered it was a 'screw', scared to death of losing respect. By saving Morris, Sid proved he was his own man. And in spite of his previously crime-filled life and anti-authority attitude, when it came to the crunch he was still capable of spontaneously lending a hand to a fellow human being in need. Was that such a bad thing?

Ron Schofield obviously thinks so, even though Sid got out years ago – and as far as I know hasn't been back in since. Maybe it's me, but so much that appears to matter in prison just doesn't seem to figure on the outside. The more time I spend on the other side of the fence, the less relevant prison attitudes are becoming. The next time I see Ron I'll try to talk to him, and see if I can get him to understand that.

4 March 2004

Cry Freedom

[This article flagged the screening of a series of prison movies over the following weekend by London's National Film Theatre]

Prison movies always go down well in prison – which is odd, you might think, given that most people watch films to escape from the

130

familiar for an hour or two, or to gain a little insight into an unfamiliar world. But it's a fact. And as far as most of those behind bars are concerned, the best prison films invariably involve the convict triumphing against adversity, winning against insurmountable odds, and beating the system. Could there be a more seductive tale for the otherwise faceless and voiceless prison community?

In reality, the chances of beating the system are slim. We all know that. But a good prison film can bring life to a prisoner's dreams. For only a prisoner knows how much courage it takes to get through even a day in prison, never mind a whole sentence – which is why prisoners find it so satisfying when this is revealed for all the world in a big film production.

Perhaps the best known example is *The Shawshank Redemption*, Frank Darabont's superlative film of Stephen King's most famous novella. How apt then that London's National Film Theatre should kick off its Prison Film Weekend tonight with a screening of this modern classic.

As most film-lovers already know, *The Shawshank Redemption* tells the story of New England banker Andy Dufresne (played with great intelligence by Tim Robbins), who is wrongly convicted and condemned, in 1945, to serve two back-to-back life terms in Shawshank prison for the murder of his wife and her lover. Dufresne's story is narrated by Red, Shawshank's 'man who can get you anything' (possibly Morgan Freeman's finest performance). When we first meet Red, he's already done a twenty-year stretch. He's still hopeful though – which is why he tells the parole-panel chairman he's been 'rehabilitated', when the question is posed during his twenty-year stage hearing. 'Oh yes, sir,' he says. 'I can honestly say I'm a changed man. God's honest truth. Absolutely rehabilitated.'

When his application is rejected, Red leaves the room and just before joining his comrades back on the yards he stops and takes a glance at the big walls around him. For a moment, we get to share the weight on his shoulders. Then he adjusts his cap, shrugs and strides back into the mêlée, his unspoken courage burning off the screen.

131

At first Red feels sorry for Dufresne. He knows what it takes to get through Shawshank and is convinced Dufresne is not going to make it. But as he observes how the former banker learns to adapt to this other cynical environment – surviving the attentions of Boggs, the homosexual rapist, or trading valuable income tax information with the sadistic head warder for a case of beer after a hot day spreading roof pitch – Red grows to respect Dufresne and to admire his spirit. As they combat the worst aspects of penal servitude together over the next twenty years, sucking blood from a thousand minor victories, the two men become firm friends.

But there's even greater glory to come at the end. When Dufresne breaks out, with a little assistance from Red, he leaves behind a clever mess that leads to the arrest of the amoral prison warden; and Red finally gets his parole at the forty-year stage, after telling the parole board that he no longer gives a shit. Then, in a scene that promises hope for the guilty as well as the inno-cent, he joins his friend Andy on a remote beach hideaway a planet away from Shawshank. A heartbreaker if ever there was one.

The NFT presentation – which launches a nationwide initia-tive: the Prison Film Project – is not an attempt to revel in prison escape and adventure stories for their own sake. The aim is to instigate a wider reflection on issues surrounding imprisonment as a response to serious crime: an attempt to consider, says the NFT website, 'the conditions, effects and value of incarceration as a method of trying to punish and, presumably, prevent crime'.

It's an admirable idea. But I couldn't help smiling when I read that the main purpose was to 'ask a few crucial questions', includ-ing, 'What is prison life like? What does it do to people? How exactly does it serve society?' With record numbers of prisoners packed into the nation's jails and a prison system trundling along in a perpetual state of near-crisis, how can it be that we still lack answers to those simple questions? Is it because society simply does not want to know? If that is the case, then that's another good reason for prisoners to love prison films and to be thankful for directors like Darabont. For how else are society's dark secrets to be brought out into the open?

The real magic of *Shawshank* is its universal appeal. You don't have to have been to prison to understand its deep-running, beautifully juxtaposed themes: innocence and guilt, goodness and corruption, power and powerlessness, incarceration and freedom. It may be cliché-ridden, but the action is well paced and the acting inspired. And anyway, genuine prison life is more cliché-ridden. Fixers and barons, kind screws and brutes, bull queers, dodgy governors... look carefully across any prison wing during association time and you might just catch a glimpse. Though you'd have to be in the thick of it, doing real time, to know for sure who's who.

Along with the British TV series *Porridge*, Steve Buscemi's film *Animal Factory* also features in the project. It is another fine example, though a poor relation to *Shawshank*. Great character acting by Willem Dafoe as Earl Copen (again, a prison 'fixer', but one who lacks the inherent dignity of Red) and Edward Furlong as Ron Decker (another prison neophyte, but one without Dufresne's wit and adaptability) just about enables this film to work. Expectations must have been high, with a script by celebrated ex-con turned author Edward Bunker (Mr Blue in *Reservoir Dogs*) and a cast that included bit parts for Steve Buscemi, Tom Arnold and Mickey Rourke. Bunker clearly knows what he's writing about and, to add to the film's authenticity, he even makes a cameo appearance.

But *Animal Factory* is too blunt for my liking, the violence too blatant. Real prison life is more insidious. When Copen tells his comrades on the yards, 'This is my prison, everybody knows that,' I'm not convinced. While the relationships, particularly that between Copen and Decker, are persuasively ambiguous, the prison journey is insufficiently defined. Con-life junkies will love its hardcore content and uncompromising bleakness, but the only time it moved me was when Copen failed, at the end, to make the breakout that was supposed to be a joint effort between him and Decker. Whoever Bunker used as the role model for Decker, and I strongly suspect the character was based on somebody he knew in prison, he must have had balls of steel to chance such an audacious escape attempt – to jump in the back of a garbage-crushing truck with just hope and a steel pole to jam the hydraulics. There it is again: that old prisoner courage.

Also worth a watch are the two classic Alan Clarke commentaries on marginalized British youth and adolescent dysfunction. *Scum* brought Ray Winstone to the big screen with a bang as borstal boy Trainee 4737 Carlin, whose intelligent use of violence (wielding pool balls in socks, for example) soon makes him the 'the daddy' of the institution. *Made in Britain* has sixteen-year-old skinhead Trevor (Tim Roth) fighting everything and everybody, but to what end? Like many naturally bright but socially disadvantaged young men, Trevor is rebelling, but I'm not sure that even he knows against what. What we do know is that he and Trainee 4737 Carlin, along with thousands of kids like them, are headed in the same direction if the cycle isn't broken early enough: penal institutions for youngsters, then penal institutions for adults. It's as true now as it was more than twenty years ago when both films were made. Yet still we are unable to answer the main question posed by this film project: how exactly does prison serve society?

But at least the question is being asked, and so long as that remains the case, we can continue to hope that one day we might develop a system that works in the best interests of all.

5 March 2004

A stranger inside and out

One of the first things Nadia said to me on the phone the other week – after she had congratulated me on being offered her old job as group coordinator – was, 'Do you feel more legit now?'

It was a good question. She obviously understood my situation pretty well. Once the exhilaration of being on the other side of the fence had eased off – and that must have taken more than a year – I found myself feeling a little unsure about my role out there. Was I really acclimatizing in preparation for a return to the ranks of the general public? The problem was that, before my life in prison, I had never felt a part of what was going on in society. Rather than returning, it felt more as if I was preparing to join society for the first time.

It is so odd sometimes, this prison life in open conditions. All this in, out, in, out. The longer it goes on, the more havoc it plays with my sense of belonging. Nadia hit the nail squarely on the head with her comment about feeling legit. It wasn't something that I had been dwelling on, but once I got the new job there was a definite feeling of being even closer to real life.

What I am discovering now is that the closer to real life I am getting, the more it feels as if I am existing in some kind of no man's land. I am neither in the one place nor the other. I never thought that I would have a problem being detached from the prison environment, as long as I was anchored firmly somewhere in the free world. But most of the time out there I still feel like a stranger.

I leave the prison early in the morning, at 6.45, long before most residents have made the first stirrings towards getting up. Along with another half-dozen early starters I check in at the house office, show my licence (which permits me to be let out) and get my name and room number booked off on the computer records.

We all make our way to the bottom of the block stairs and wait for the operational support officer to come and unlock the back door. While we wait we hang our heads, stare out of the reinforced-glass door panel, crack half-hearted jokes or comment on the weather – anything to pass those long few minutes until the key is in the door and we can file out into the morning air. That is always such a good feeling.

It feels even better when we are marching out of the gate five or six minutes later. After handing in our room keys to the gate officer, and showing his assistant our licences, the small gate is swung open and out we go. Spirits are always high at that point.

No heads hanging. Just bustle and genuine smiles. In the car park we split and go our own ways. That is the best part of all.

Although it takes exactly the same time – give or take the type of rain or snow or leaves on the line – the train journey to work seems shorter than it used to. That is because there is so much more to think about in my new job. Switching off is hard. But the job is going well, I think.

I am about a quarter of the way up the steep learning curve that I knew I would have to scale when I started. It is an adequate performance, I suppose, although I thought I would be higher up the curve by now. I assured the panel at my interview that I was a fast learner. Even though the hours are long, my days pass quickly as the brain works overtime, reading files, organizing logistics, taking calls, keeping the office ticking over. I am learning fast. I just hope it is fast enough.

I like to get away from my desk and out of the office for a coffee or an iced tea around one thirty or two o'clock – if there's time. Thought-collecting moments are rare. On the train back to prison, I work: reading reports, jotting notes, drafting letters. It is having an effect. Late one evening last week, in a sleepy daze, I got off the train a stop too soon. Instead of waiting an hour for the next train – which would have meant getting back even later than the usual nine thirty – I ordered a cab.

'Where to?' asked the driver.

He gave me a funny look when I told him I wanted to go to the next station. My car was covered in frost. I scraped the windows and drove back to the prison. Behind the fence once more, the buildings are familiar. In the house-block, I see one or two familiar faces. My room is familiar. But I'm feeling like a stranger.

11 March 2004

Office-hunting in the city

Responsibilities have been coming thick and fast during these first few weeks in my new job. In the grand scheme of things, most would seem relatively banal to the average professional, I guess: writing cheques, logging time sheets, arranging volunteer schedules and so on. But after so many years on prison wings and landings with few responsibilities, it is hard not to credit my new duties with a greater importance than they would merit in other circumstances.

As I make my way towards what I hope is the end of my prison time, I'm becoming more and more aware of how decisions we all make and actions we all take impact directly on those around us. When I applied for the job it was because I wanted to bring what I could to the organization. I wanted to put the strengths I had developed in prison at its disposal. After expending so much energy, and withstanding such a variety of pressures with little that was positive to show for it, I was keen to be in a position to have a beneficial effect. The job has given me that position. I hope that now I can live up to the trust placed in me.

It's one thing to imagine how you would perform in a role that isn't actually yours, like being an armchair soldier or politician. It's easy to make decisions that will never be tested. But once you're in the driving seat, it's another matter. I'm anxious, I suppose, that's all. Not for myself, but for the others in the organization who are going to be affected by my successes or failures. When I applied for the job, I was as certain as I've ever been that I was ready for this challenge. But the proof will be in the results, in, say, six months', or a year's time.

Yet there is no sense of anxiety in the office. I said I could do it and so I'm expected to get on with it. When Phoebe announced the other week that the organization was now in a position to recruit another full-time person, everybody was thrilled. The new post is for a specialized worker, and the successful applicant will be able to provide much assistance to many vulnerable people.

The only drawback is that the office is not very big. Getting another workstation in place is going to be a squeeze. 'I know,' said Phoebe when this was pointed out. 'That's why we're going to have to move to a bigger office.' Turning to me and smiling,

Phoebe added, 'And that will be your responsibility.'

'Er, of course,' I said. 'Fine. I'll get on with it straight away.'

I'd be lying if I said that at that moment my heart did not miss a beat. Outwardly, however, I remained calm. As I panned the open-plan room I thought hard as I caught the eye of each of my colleagues. An intelligent-sounding question was in order, I decided. 'Do we have any preferences with regard to area?' I asked. As I waited for a response, all I could think of was: where the hell do I start?

Talk about learning fast. Phoebe said that my primary concern should be cost. From my reading of the accounts I already knew we were not bursting at the seams with spare cash – we are a charity after all. 'We need more space,' said Phoebe, 'but for less rent.' My brief could not have been clearer.

Somehow I'd picked up the idea that estate agents are a shifty bunch. After randomly selecting a few that specialize in business premises from the phone book, I made my first, guarded, call.

'Hello?' said a friendly voice.

'Hello,' I said. 'I'm enquiring about renting some office space.'

The voice became warmer. He used my first name and talked about 'square feet... blah blah, service charges... blah blah, break clause... blah blah.' I made what I thought were knowing sounds in the right places and eventually managed to stop him and tell him I'd get back to him later. The fact of the matter was that for most of the conversation I hadn't a clue what he was talking about.

I'm glad to report now, however, that since then I've made some progress. Now, I too can talk fast on the phone. I can guess the size of floor space to within fifty square feet or so – and if anybody tells me that rents are cheaper 'south of the river', I can tell them with authority 'not necessarily'.

The good news is I've found four premises that I believe could meet our needs. Viewings have been arranged. Fingers crossed, my colleagues will be pleased – my first big responsibility to be put to the test.

18 March 2004

Ron's problem

I'd forgotten all about Ron Schofield. We'd blanked each other a couple of times following our spat the other weekend over the merits of fellow con Sid Fearlittle saving a prison officer's life years ago. But by Monday morning the matter had dropped to the bottom of my 'things that deserve serious attention' list. I'd catch up with Ron again eventually, I surmised, once he'd settled in to this open regime and got used to the idea that he could now leave behind the hardcore prison culture if he wanted to.

The difference between open- and closed-prison conditions is vast, and different people respond to the change in different ways. The response is most marked, I believe, in those who have served the longest sentences. For me the experience was emotional. Accepting a kindness was the most difficult. Of course, I had been shown kindness in the prisons that I had been in previously, but here it seemed to be intrinsic to the general attitude. I'd never come across such a concentration of helpful prison officers before. From the day I landed, when the two reception officers helped me carry my bags to my room, right up until it was time for me to go outside the fence unaccompanied, I've had nothing but assistance from this unusual breed of custodians.

It's a situation that is not easy to accept for somebody who has been used to the mostly debilitating attitudes that prevail in the closed prisons. Ron had been in the closed system for even longer than my near twenty-year stretch. Which was why I'd decided I'd make the effort to talk to Ron once we'd had time to reflect on the silliness of our argument. We would run into one another again soon enough – it's always the way in these places. Have a fall-out with someone and you're guaranteed to keep bumping into them when you least expect it: you'll be going up the stairs and they'll be coming down; you'll be heading down the narrowest part of a corridor, they'll be coming up it. Though with me being out of the jail for most of the week these days, I thought it would be a while longer before me and

Ron would get the chance to have another natter.

On days in I always try to get out for a run. Long days in the office and short weekends (and the low fear factor that accompanies life in open-prison conditions) has meant that my formerly rigorous keep-fit-and-strong routine has all but been abandoned. But I haven't given up on the running. The lower compound is usually empty when the weather is bad, as it was last Sunday afternoon. As I sauntered down in shorts, T-shirt and tracksuit top the hail began bouncing off the tarmac path.

Just as my knees were beginning to turn blue I noticed the donkey jacket-clad figure sitting hunched on the low dry-stone wall a few feet inside the compound gates. Rain joined the hail and I had to squint through the grey gusts, but it wasn't until I was close up that I recognized him – looking like he was brooding over something or other.

'Ron,' I said as I stepped through the gates. 'How's it going?'

I couldn't believe it when he appeared to blank me again.

'Oi,' I said. 'Are you ignoring me or what? I said, "How's it going?"'

Still he continued to stare out past the fence and over the rolling fields. Annoyed with myself for giving in to him, I was just about to take off my tracksuit top and say 'bollocks' before jogging off, when he spoke.

'I can't get over how far you can see over there.'

Instantly my mood changed back to conciliatory. 'I know,' I said.

'It keeps hitting me. All those years... gone.'

'They're better off gone,' I said. 'Now's the time for new beginnings.' Ron still hadn't looked up at me. Eventually he did.

'I just can't believe I've made it to a place like this. I keep looking back and thinking, "What the fuck was that all about?"'

'Ron,' I said, 'I was exactly the same. But it's best not to dwell on it. Try and adjust as quickly as you can. Then use it to get yourself ready for out there. That's what it's for. They'll help you here.'

Much as I love being out in inclement weather, I really had to get moving before the whole of me turned blue. It was enough that Ron and I had agreed to continue our talk later. After second thoughts I kept my top on and off I trotted. By the time I'd finished pounding my ten laps under the wind-driven sleet, he was gone.

25 March 2004

Panic on the Number 9

One of the most enjoyable parts of looking for new offices for the charity I work for was the chance to wander further afield than my journey to and from work normally allows. Much as I love my commute – the train, the walk through the city, the blending in unnoticed among crowds of fellow taxpayers – I've become much more aware of how limited my movements are each time I make the trip outside the fence.

I haven't felt particularly restricted, although officially I am. Normally I'm so preoccupied with work matters anyway that I hardly get around to thinking about what lies beyond. I've been content just to look around my immediate vicinity, so often amazed at what I can see now that I'm looking through different eyes.

For no reason other than a colleague's suggestion that the rents might be cheaper, my first expedition took me south of the river. I was all geared up for it, enthusiastic, confident and optimistic – until the damned bus ride. I should have been prepared, but it didn't dawn on me until the double-decker was pulling up that I couldn't remember the last time I had ridden on one. It seems ridiculous now but I couldn't remember the procedure. Asking one of the three people in the queue in front of me was out of the question at that stage, though it did occur to me momentarily to put on an accent and pretend I was an asylum seeker.

Perhaps the conductor would assist, I thought, as I stepped on board and attempted to follow the others. I didn't get far.

'Excuse me,' said the driver before I got past his cab. I nodded towards the people in front. 'They've got travelcards,' he said. 'Where are you going?'

'Er, south of the river,' I mumbled, now acutely aware of the collective gaze in my direction from all those on the packed lower deck.

'Where south of the river?' In my rising panic I couldn't think where exactly.

'Er, the first stop at the other side of the bridge,' I said.

'£1,' said the driver.

After handing over my coin and taking the ticket from the machine I headed upstairs, desperate to get out of sight of the downstairs passengers. The upper deck was pretty full, too, but I managed to plonk down beside an elderly woman and began to relax again. It had been a while since I had felt so strongly like an alien out there and the experience threw me. During the ride the spectacular view helped to take my mind off my anxiety, especially the view across the water. But as we reached the other side, panic returned. How did a person get off? By pressing the bell of course. But where was it? And should I press once, or twice?

With heart beating and back sweating, I scrambled down to the bottom of the stairs only to find a couple already standing by the exit doors, waiting to disembark. The woman pressed the bell on the upright pole and, a minute later, the bus pulled to a halt and the doors swung open. I had never imagined that just stepping off a bus could generate such feelings of pleasure – and relief.

The incident undermined my confidence for the rest of the day. My plan had been to call a few numbers from estate agent advertising boards above commercial premises and try to get a feel for negotiating in such matters.

I knew I would have to learn fast but the first call I made turned out to be a disaster. I stuttered and stumbled over my words, 'Er, not sure how many square feet. Service charge – what's that? Break clause? Not sure...' I imagined the slick professional on the other end sniggering at my ineptitude.

Thankfully, I recovered. Within days I was negotiating like an old hand. (A good technique I found was to imagine that the estate agents I talked to were wearing blue-and-white striped convict shirts. Weird, I know, but it helped to negate my status anxiety.) My colleagues had no idea. They liked the four properties I eventually short-listed for viewing, glad that we were staying this side of the river. The office we settled on had a third more floor space than the one we had to leave, and the rent was £2,000 a year less – with the first three months rent-free. I'm pleased to report that we've just moved in. The 'well dones' and 'congratulations' have been numerous and heartfelt. Everybody seems happy, including me. But that bus thing was scary.

8 April 2004

Breakfast with the law

One of the things that has struck me since I have been coming out of jail regularly on my own is the amount of freedom that still exists in our society. As long as I drive carefully, pay for my train ticket and conduct myself in a reasonable manner whenever I am out, nobody pays me any mind. Not once during my comings and goings, for example, have I been stopped by the police and asked where I have come from or where I am going. It feels natural, but I am a long way from taking it for granted.

I remember the first time I came across a policeman in the street. Tall, helmeted and wearing a fluorescent yellow jacket over his tunic, he was standing by a pedestrian crossing, and his eyes were on the traffic at a busy intersection a few yards up. He was talking into the radio on his lapel, and as I got closer I felt my heart begin to beat faster. The reason for my sudden anguish was unclear at first. He was not even looking in my direction. Then as I was about to pass him, he turned and caught my eye.

'Morning,' I said, with a forced look of what I hoped was non-chalance on my reddening, sweating face.

'Morning, sir,' he replied.

143

There was no logical reason for me to be anxious in his presence. But, not wanting to arouse his suspicions, once I had passed him I did not look back. I liked being Mr Anonymous and I wanted it to stay that way. Afterwards, I wondered about my odd reaction and reasoned that it must have been simply because it was the first time I had been so close to a policeman since I went to prison. There was obviously a remnant of a bad memory lingering not too deep in my subconscious.

I have never had anything against the police personally and there is no reason for them to have anything against me now. In fact if anything, in what must be an example of the height of irony, I have become accustomed to feeling a sense of comfort whenever I see a policeman in the vicinity. After living for so long in a controlled environment, the lack of overt control on the outside, though much appreciated, can be unnerving. None of this was on my mind the other morning, however, when I went out searching for a cheap place to eat lunch.

It had been a long morning. No breakfast – nothing packed from the prison. (As much as I am grateful for free prison food, I have reached the point where I cannot face another corned-beef sandwich.) So I searched the area near where I work for a downmarket, greasy spoon type of place that might provide an all-day breakfast for under a fiver. It did not take long.

The windows were steamed up, but I could see through the streaks that the place was busy. The menu on the door displayed the kind of prices I was looking for, so in I went. Almost immediately the short, Italian-looking and sounding lady behind the counter placed herself opposite me. 'Yes please?'

I glanced up at the blackboard fry-up. 'Today's special please.'

'Beans or tomatoes?'

'Both,' I said, and handed over my £5 note.

As she opened the till and called the order through to the cook, I looked around for a place to sit. It was busier than I had realized. A waitress beckoned to me. 'Here,' she said, smiling, and guided me between the chattering, chomping diners to the back and around a large pillar to an empty table for two. I felt lucky until it dawned on me that the group of builders on the next table were not builders – but six fluorescent-jacketed police officers.

I can't deny it was a shock. But I kept cool and took my seat as the old nonchalance routine kicked in again. They would probably have had a bigger shock if they had known my circumstances, I thought. As I waited for my fry-up it was impossible not to overhear their conversation. Another shock. Instead of discussing crime figures or collars felt, the main topic seemed to be the merits of the Atkins diet. According to the most portly among them, it allowed for large portions of sausage and bacon to be eaten regularly. His plate was empty so I couldn't say how big the portions were that he was talking about. Mentally, I raised an eyebrow. Moments later they downed the dregs of tea from their mugs and were gone.

As I walked back to the office, I thought about the differences between us. On the one hand they appear huge – on the other, perhaps they are not so great.

15 April 2004

No parole for Larrson

As far as I could see there was nothing else Larrson could have done to prove himself. When his parole application failed late last year, most people here were surprised. While it's true that being in open conditions is not enough in itself to guarantee a favourable result from the parole board, generally speaking, so long as you're doing what you're supposed to be doing and not coming to the attention of the authorities for any nefarious conduct, a positive answer is the norm rather than the exception.

From what I saw during my admittedly sporadic association with Larrson during his early months here, I thought he was as strong a candidate as any for an early release. I had seen him pull away from his group of rowdy pals – young men to whom he had been powerfully connected by a shared history of young offenders' institutions – yet keep their respect. That took some doing.

One day, he was standing next to me in the meal queue when somebody asked him, 'So what are you then – a con's man or a screw's man?' Larrson looked his questioner in the eye and said, 'Neither. I'm my own man.' Shame there wasn't a member of the parole board lurking who could have witnessed that display of inner strength. Being your own man in prison is hard enough even for older hands. For younger men it is often their biggest challenge.

There were other signs that Larrson was developing a consistently responsible attitude. His first job in the prison as an orderly in the gym meant he had to set the pace in strength and fitness. His lean frame was soon rippling, but I never heard of him using his physical presence to get his own way with those weaker than him. The PE staff liked him, too, but not once did I hear tales that he had been laughing at their jokes or making their tea.

When he helped out at the prison's annual party for local pensioners the Christmas before last, his polite manner (always addressing the elderly folk as 'sir' and 'madam') and tireless fetching and carrying of food and drink ensured that the guests went away with a view of young men in prison that would not normally be available to them.

I saw less of Larrson once he started paid work. I didn't know what his job was until the Celtic Poet told me it was something to do with protecting the environment. I would have thought a job like that needed a notable measure of commitment. He must have been working outside for a good six months when he reached his first parole eligibility date. That should have been long enough for an observer to judge that he had developed a strong work ethic, considering it was the first time in his life that he had had regular employment. In Larrson's case, I think the parole board missed an opportunity that first time around.

To his credit, he stayed cool. 'I'm trying to change for me, and for my mum,' he told me after his knock-back. 'Not for the parole board.' Like his mother, I guess, Larrson was hoping he would be out early. She would have seen, heard and read about the progress he was making during visits and in his letters. After what he had achieved she must have felt entitled to expect his release after his first review. The fact that it didn't happen probably affected her more than it did him.

I expect his mother is feeling anxious again now. Last Friday Larrson stopped me on my way in to the dining hall. It was a cold, bright day and the sunshine was bouncing off his freshly shaved head. I correctly adduced that the worried look on his face had something to do with the bulging yellow folder under his arm. 'They're in there,' he said, pointing to the door of the adjacent building normally used to house visits.

I hadn't spoken to him for weeks and didn't know what he was talking about. 'Who?' I said.

'The parole panel. I'm waiting to go in to present my case.'

Before I could say anything, the visits door opened and he was called in. I managed a quick call of 'Good luck', then he disappeared inside.

It turned out that this parole hearing had been brought forward – a good sign. They told him his last application failed because he hadn't done enough 'offending-behaviour work'. When I saw him on Friday night he was upbeat. 'They were smiling when I left,' he said. For his sake, I hope that was a good sign too. He'll know for sure by the end of the month.

22 April 2004

What Ron did to Sid

I believe that, if they have the need and desire, most people can change the way they live if they really put their minds to it. In prison the need is usually greater than on the outside. But it's not enough just to talk about it. To succeed, it takes massive effort, which is why I baulked when I overheard one prison officer telling another a while ago that the only reason Ron Schofield had made it to open conditions was that about three years ago, after more than twenty years inside, he had sat and persuaded a governor that he'd changed. 'He cried,' I heard the officer say. Well, forgive me for being sceptical.

The truth is, many years ago Ron and I knew each other a little more than I've been letting on. He was a very heavy figure in the jail we were in. He was feared by many, and not without good reason. He and I were on nodding terms, but only because conflict between us would have been too dangerous. So we kept our distance and kept our peace – at least until Ron's latter days in the place.

At the heart of our contretemps when it occurred was a man called Tetchy who was Ron's 'joey' (a weak prisoner who acts as a stronger person's gofer in return for protection). One day Tetchy was found in severe distress and taken to the hospital wing to recuperate. It so happened that the hospital orderly was Sid Fearlittle, the one who had saved a prison officer's life in his last prison. Sid lived in the hospital full time and, apart from when he had to drop off appointment slips, hardly ever ventured onto the main wing.

Sid knew there was gossip concerning his life-saving act and that there were those who would do him harm because of it. But it wasn't fear that kept him off the wing: he'd changed his attitude after saving the officer and all he wanted to do was to get to the open jail he'd been promised and then go home.

Anyway, on the Sunday morning following Tetchy's admission the governor was doing his rounds and as usual checked in at the hospital. The escorting officer opened Tetchy's cell door and before the governor could even say, 'How are we feeling this morning?' Tetchy jumped him. The officer steamed in but Tetchy went berserk and the struggle became fierce. At some point the commotion woke Sid, who slept in the open ward and had been having a lie-in. Still half asleep, Sid pulled on shorts and ambled towards the racket. Faced with the violent entanglement he reacted instinctively – and pressed the alarm bell. The cavalry arrived and carted Tetchy away, which is when the real trouble started.

Once in the segregation block, Tetchy told everybody that Sid hadn't just pressed the bell, but that he'd then grabbed him, twisted his arm up his back and held him until the mufti squad got there. There were no independent witnesses, but as soon as this 'news' reached the wing the baying for Sid's scalp began in earnest. Tetchy, in the meantime, was shipped out – which I suspect was all he wanted in the first place.

I didn't believe the arm-twisting bit. I knew that Sid had changed his way of thinking and had turned his back on the prison culture, but he hadn't gone bananas. So I was curt with anybody who tried to tell me the tale – and that included Schofield. 'He's a fucking wrong 'un,' said Ron.

'No Ron,' I said. 'He might have pressed the bell, but the other stuff is complete garbage and you know it.' When the contract was put out on Sid I went to Ron's cell and told him straight what I thought.

'So you're with him then?' he said.

'Yes I am,' I said.

Understandably, prison staff had a soft spot for Sid. When they heard about the contract, Ron was 'ghosted' (snatched by the mufti-squad after night-time bang-up and taken to a waiting van for a trip to HMP Unknown). Soon afterwards Sid went to an open jail and that was the end of the matter – except Ron had left a few poisonous whispers on the wing about me.

Nine years later, Ron lands here. He knew I knew what he'd done. But there was no apology, no acknowledgement of mistakes made, and no embarrassment expressed about past actions. Instead, the first thing Ron did when we spoke was to start slagging off Sid. No change there then.

In the circumstances I suppose I should have been nonplussed when I got in from work the other night and found that Ron was gone. In the end he couldn't handle the open regime, he'd said, and demanded to be returned to the closed system. In my heart of hearts I felt sorry for him. But the choice had been his.

29 April 2004

Tank and Albert

A letter from Tank came as a nice surprise this week. I recognized his uneven print on the envelope immediately, but when I opened it the first thing I noted was the date: hard to believe that a year had passed since the big man had been released.

He was writing in his articulated truck, he said, 'from a lay-by in Northampton'. It was good to know he was still working anyway. I hadn't forgotten the concerns he had had about getting out. After losing his job in the factory for being a mite too vocal about unsatisfactory working conditions, he had been lucky to have the chance to retrain as an HGV driver. The new skill gave him an immediate focus and he had been elated to land his first driving job while still in prison.

I worried about my pal though, as I knew that many of the problems he had had on the outside and which had contributed to his several years in jail were still unresolved. He had hinted about his fears, and when the time came for him to get out I knew they were real.

The morning of a prisoner's release is an intense time. Few sleep well the night before. Most are up early, showered, shaved, and ready to go hours before the prison comes awake. When I went to say goodbye to Tank on his liberty morning he was still in bed, his great hairy head deep under the covers – obviously a man not overly keen to face whatever awaited him in the free world. To me that buried head said more than words ever could.

As I continued to read his letter I became alarmed by his apparent tone of disappointment with life outside. For most of the past year he had been on the road six days a week, eating at truck stops and bedding down in his lorry's sleeper compartment. It sounded like a tough life – albeit one that thousands of others have to make the best of. I found myself whispering, 'Come on amigo – lift up.' When I got to the part where he said, 'Some days I've longed to be back inside, as the cab has felt as lonely as a cell,' I wanted to shout out loud.

I had had a long day in the office and I was tired. Finding Tank's letter on my bed when I got in had lifted my spirits. He had been a man with potential and I had hoped for good news. I read on.

He explained that he had been staying at his parents' house a couple of weekends ago when there had been a knock at the door. Tank's mother answered and brought the caller into the room where my massive mucker sat watching *Coronation Street*. 'Son,' she said, 'it's Dorian.'

Now Dorian was the person to whom Tank's parents had given Albert, his beloved bull terrier, after Tank had gone to prison. I could imagine Tank's feelings at Dorian's appearance. He had mentioned the name often during our many walks and talks, and while he understood that Albert had been too much for his elderly parents to cope with, there were occasions when he expressed more than a tad of resentment towards Dorian. 'I just hope he's looking after Albert properly,' he had said a number of times, sometimes with a growl and a shake of the head. Yet I believe that deep down he was grateful Dorian had adopted Albert. It had either been that, or the long goodnight.

For Tank, Dorian's arrival out of the blue could mean only one thing. 'My heart sank,' he wrote, 'for I knew that Albert had passed away and that Dorian had come because he thought I should know. But before I could say anything to him he started to talk about his domestic problems, about leaving his wife and finding someone new. I just sat in silence wondering why he was telling me all this. Then he said, "So I've had to move to a smaller flat and I can't take Albert with me. I wonder if you would please take him back?"'

Tank's joy then sang from the page. My spirits were lifted at last. 'The prospect of being reunited with my one true friend was too wonderful for words.' Hoorah! I thought, there was good news after all. 'I never thought I'd see Albert again. But now he's curled up beside me as I write and I'm a happy trucker again.'

He signed off wishing me well and calling me his good buddy. Bedtime came and as I drifted off to sleep with an image of Tank and Albert travelling the highways together I was smiling, gladdened by the knowledge that the loneliness of the long-distance ex-con was over.

6 May 2004

Sad Joe's second chance

Larrson walked last week. I didn't even know he had had his answer from the parole board until Joe Fales told me. Fales stopped me as I stepped out of the library after browsing through the papers on Sunday morning and started to talk about his own case again. 'I'm down for an oral hearing in June,' he said. 'They've got to let me go this time, haven't they?' I knew he was fishing for reassurance but, to tell you the truth, I wasn't in the mood to give it.

There's no denying that Fales has had a raw deal. It's taken him almost five years to get to this position again after being sent back to the closed system for twice failing alcometer tests during his first stint in open conditions. It seemed a stiff punishment for what was, strictly speaking, no more than a breach of prison rules. But since his original offence – the 'index offence' – was alcohol-related, the authorities probably felt obliged to take a more serious view of his transgression. And anyway, the sending back was not just supposed to be a punishment. He was told to undertake an alcohol-education course and perhaps an enhanced thinking skills course, and any other course that might help him to take a more responsible attitude to his conduct in the future.

But his problems deepened once he was back in the closed system as none of the officials he met considered him to be a priority case. There are so many people in prison now, the majority of whom are trying to get on courses in order to fulfil sentence-plan requirements and impress the parole board, that once you have had your chance and fail, you go straight to the back of the queue. For a lifer the queue is non-negotiable. The only option is to pester and push until somebody relents. Fales was lucky it only took him four years to get back to open conditions.

While he was away from the open system, there was a new development in the way life-sentenced prisoners are considered for release. Lifers can now opt for an 'oral hearing', in which they appear in person in front of a parole panel to argue their case. The advantage is that the parole board can see you as a fellow human being rather than just as a series of typed sheets of paper. In my own case there was nothing contentious in my reports so I said I was happy just to have a 'paper hearing'.

Fales says that when he gets his chance he's going to tell them that he's had enough. 'I'm going to give them some home truths,' he said on Sunday. I believe he wanted me to remonstrate with him, to tell him not to be unwise, to prepare properly, to think carefully about what he was going to say on the day. Instead I said, 'Well, if you think that's going to get you out, go ahead and do it.' The fact is that almost no matter what Fales tells the parole panel, so long as he doesn't go berserk and attack one of them during the hearing, the odds are he's going to stroll it. I think they would be too embarrassed to keep him in any longer. Although you never can tell. Look what happened to Larrson first time around.

Fales was encouraged by Larrson's success. 'I think they want people out. They're running out of room. That's why they brought Larrson's second review forward.'

'Maybe,' I said, though I doubted it. They certainly want people out, but not at any cost. Larrson should have been out six months ago. I think somebody must have thought they were in danger of losing him if they didn't consider his case again quickly. Fales should have been back in open conditions at least two years ago. But, as I said, once you fail you're no longer considered a priority.

I nodded at Fales, said I would see him later and then went for a walk around the football field. All the talk about 'answers' and 'hearings' got me thinking about my own situation. A memo was shoved under my door at the beginning of March telling me that my reports had been sent to the parole board for my release to be considered. My answer must be due any day now. It's been a long time getting to this stage, and I don't know how I'm going to feel if I actually get a release date at last. If I do, it will be a relief not to have to keep coming back to prison after a day's work. The pressure of living two lives is wearying. But I'm not anxious to be given freedom. In my head I found that for myself years ago.

13 May 2004

First-class citizens

Rarely a week goes by without some uncomfortable incident or other occurring on the train during my journey back to the prison after a day at work. The other evening, my train was packed as usual as it pulled away from the city station. A man in shorts, T-shirt and cap had been standing on the platform several paces to the side and behind me, drinking a can of lager and talking at a hands-free mobile phone. That looked odd for a start. I turned and observed discreetly as he laughed, swore and gesticulated into the air, all the while punctuating his conversation with swigs from his can. His heavily pregnant partner stood close by, guarding a large upright suitcase and holding a fishing rod that I assumed was his as he kept breaking off his chat to tell her to 'keep it off the ground'.

When the train stopped and the doors opened, I was glad I was at the front of the mêlée. My instinct told me that it would not take much to antagonize lager man, so I needed to make sure that once we were in the carriage there was distance between us. As the doors closed and the whistle sounded, I bagged one of the few seats left and then suddenly there was a roar, 'Oi! Don't push her out of the way, she's fackin' pregnant!'

Through legs and past elbows, I could see that lager man had brought the fishing rod on board (leaving his partner with two hands so she could haul in the suitcase). A man with a tan, wearing beige slacks and a navy blazer, had tripped over the rod and barged into the woman. 'I didn't push her!' tanned man howled.

'Well, watch where you're fackin' going,' said lager man and mumbled something I couldn't make out. He and his partner then shuffled through the door leading to the adjoining carriage and just before the doors closed I heard him say, 'Prick.'

By then tanned man was sitting in the only empty seat left, which happened to be directly opposite me, and couldn't help but hear the remark too. Once the dividing door was closed tanned man replied, 'Wally.'

I hadn't heard that one for a few years. With an embarrassed smile, he looked about for some acknowledgement that he was the injured party, but received none. Nobody wanted to get involved.

The ruckus between tanned man and lager man was barely over when again there were raised voices from the first-class section, where a couple had sat down by mistake.

'We didn't notice,' said the woman.

'I'm sorry,' said a male voice, 'but these are the regulations.'

Regulations? Along with several others I craned my neck to see what was going on. The couple were smartly dressed – to me they looked 'professional'. The woman was the more distressed, and more vocal. 'But it wasn't obvious...'

I had never seen more than one member of train staff in a carriage at one time. Now there were three – all bearing down on the couple.

The woman had a point. The train was a quiet, modern type, with sliding doors, plush upholstery and tables between seats. Compared to the old rattling stock, every carriage feels and, indeed, looks like a first-class compartment. 'First class' is just sixteen seats partitioned at one end of the carriage with different-coloured upholstery. I sat there in error myself once. When I was asked for my ticket and the error was spotted, I apologized and was allowed to move. No hassle. But this couple were definitely being hassled.

With details logged, they ended up standing by the door looking most unhappy. I couldn't help thinking that they had been treated with such discourtesy because they were black. The three officials were white. At the next stop it became apparent that others might have seen it that way too. A white woman getting off said to the couple, 'Excuse me, are you going to complain?'

'Yes. I think we must,' said the man.

'Well, here's my card, please call if you need support.'

I could see emotion in the black woman's eyes and I felt a little bit choked myself. Then a white man chipped in, 'You've got my support too' – then another, and then another white woman. I kept quiet, but it was reassuring to see so many others recognizing that there are times when not getting 'involved' is not really an option.

20 May 2004

My parole answer

It had been lurking in the pit of my stomach for a while. I'd be lying if I said it hadn't. I'm talking about the tad of anxiety concerning the answer to my parole application. From the moment I was told in March that my reports had been sent off, I've tried to keep my thinking about the eventual response to an absolute minimum. I've seen so many people drive themselves half mad with anticipation in relation to these things. I was determined to stay cool and just focus on matters in hand – working, writing. The last thing I needed was to be distracted by whimsical notions about the possibility of having a release date at last.

Those in the know said that the normal waiting time for a lifer to get an answer is around six weeks from when the papers go off. It was as soon as that time was up that I started to consciously wonder about it. The odd thing was that I had no idea how the answer would come. Countless times I've heard people say, 'I've had my answer, blah, blah.' But I never heard anyone say, 'Great. But how did the answer arrive exactly? What form did it take?'

I noticed two or three weeks ago that I had started trying to read the faces of the gate officers for clues when I arrived back from work in the evening. But no signals were ever forthcoming. Just the usual, semi-jocular 'You still here?' when they answered the buzzer and found me waiting outside to get in. And me semi-smiling and giving my stock answer, 'Er, yeah, 'fraid so.'

In the porch I'm handed my room key, and then the night cocky lets me through the inner gate and walks me across to the house-block. We talk about the weather, he fills me in on the day's events that (thankfully) I've missed (the van driver's been sacked, Joe Bloggs has been shipped out etc., etc.). A quick 'Goodnight' and I'm turning the key and letting myself in to my room.

I suppose I was expecting a memo. Immediately I stepped inside, my eyes would scan the floor for anything official looking that might have been shoved under the door. Then the bed. The top of the cupboard, perhaps? Years ago, I took on board the phi-losophy of the experienced hands who advised, 'Expect nothing and you'll never be disappointed.' But that's easy when nobody's going anywhere, there's little on the horizon, and the light at the end of the tunnel appears to have been switched off. Now the situation could not be more different. I'm standing on the hori-zon and there is no tunnel, only light.

It must have been fatigue, but the other night when there was a development regarding 'the answer', the damn thing had com-pletely slipped my mind. Demands in the office that day had been fierce. I'd dozed on the train back. When the gate man asked me if I was still here, all I could muster was a half-hearted 'Hmm'. In the porch, the dividing window slid open and I was handed my key. It was the same old routine, until the gate man added, 'Oh, this note was on your hook.' A note? For me? In my weary brain nothing unusual registered. Not until I opened the folded paper and read the words. It was from the governor responsible for lifers. 'Please come and see me as soon as possi-ble.' That was when my heart missed a beat.

'As soon as possible'? It had to be my answer. A long night fol-lowed. Weird dreams. Long bouts of staring at the ceiling. I thought the next day was never going to arrive. Luckily it was already scheduled as a 'day in'. In the morning, I sat drinking tea until I knew the lifer governor would be in his office. Then, wouldn't you know, I bumped into him as he was on his way round there.

'Morning, governor,' I said, with well-practised nonchalance, I hoped. 'I got your note.'

'Good,' he said. 'Come with me. I've got something for you.'

As we strolled I was pleased with the way I comported myself, giving no sign of the adrenaline gushing round my insides, though my voice may have been an octave or two higher than normal.

His desk was strewn with papers. He searched for my envelope and finally found it. Could he open it any slower? 'Good news,' he said at last, handing me the letter. I read it quickly, then slowly, then slowly again. 'Your release date has been provisionally set...'

In a couple of months, when my twenty years is up, I'll be packing my kit for the last time.

3 June 2004

Church memories of an apple-stealing bishop

It is funny how, when you live a strictly regulated life, sometimes you get the urge to do something out of the ordinary. As long as you don't allow yourself to be led into trouble, I suppose a blip in the routine is allowable occasionally, even for me. That was how I found myself sitting on an old wooden bench in an ancient church a couple of mornings ago. I had been walking past on my way to work when the urge suddenly took hold. My train into the city had been on time, so I was running twenty minutes early.

I had noticed the church before. Its beautiful arched entrance sits rather incongruously alongside a bar and a fancy restaurant, and during one lunchtime walk I had ventured inside and taken a cursory look – but there had been no time to sit down, and no particular inclination.

I am not sure why I felt the need this time. It had been a long time since I had paid a proper visit to a church. Not that I had ever been a churchgoer before coming to prison. Far from it. If anyone had asked me for my view on churches and religion in those days, I would have struggled to give a reasonable answer. If anything, I thought churches were just for the good people of the world.

My first visit to a church in prison was made at the behest of Joan, the wing psychologist. In my eyes Joan epitomized what it meant to be a 'good person'. She was adamant that there was good in everybody – even in the worst of those of us fortunate enough to be on the wing where she had responsibility for psychological assessments. She even persuaded some of us that she might be right. Every few weeks she would make appointments for individual prisoners to attend meetings with her in her wing office. (How we would cringe on our return from the workshops at lunchtime to find our names chalked up on the board, followed by 'psycho call-up'. But it was a small price to pay for the help on offer.)

The interviews would last for up to two hours and took the form of informal conversations. It was only after my third or fourth session that I started to understand the process: the conversation was, in fact, a subtle mechanism by which she could explore the make-up of her subjects, unravelling complicated lives without making anyone feel unnecessarily threatened or overly vulnerable. Her skill, and compassion, enabled many people who were in the early stages of seemingly endless terms of incarceration to believe it was possible to rebuild worthwhile lives.

The only time Joan got me ruffled was when she asked me one day if I had ever considered going to the service in the prison chapel. 'It might help you to find answers,' she said. I doubted that very much. When I did eventually make the effort one Sunday morning, it was purely so that I could tell Joan, who made no secret of the fact that she was a Christian, that I had given her idea a try. It was a misguided way of showing her some gratitude, I guess.

The morning I chose happened to be the one when the local bishop was visiting. The ceremony was an interesting distraction from the usual Sunday morning routine, but nothing particularly grabbed me until the bishop took the floor and began to talk about his childhood.

'When I was a boy,' he said, 'I used to steal apples from the orchard of the cathedral where I now preside.' I thought that was a lovely story. He went on to describe the journey of his young life: the chances that came his way, those that didn't, and the choices he made – the good ones and the not so good. I'd no idea if the bishop was an especially blameless person, but his honesty about his path to self-discovery sounded too effortless to be anything less than genuine. Above all, what was clear was that he now knew who he was – and that ended up being the point of his sermon. 'Whatever brought you to this point in your life,' he concluded, 'remember that this is an opportunity to find yourself. Amen.'

Amen. The pungency of the incense in the old city church vividly brought back that memory. Joan was pleased when I told her I had been. Attending church services became a habit for a good few years afterwards and, although I never fully committed to a religious conversion, my involvement in church activities added much to my personal development. I think that was one of the reasons for my urge the other morning, and I think Joan would have been happy to know that I had not forgotten.

10 June 2004

Questions from Mr Negative

'What do you think of this place then, mate?' I was standing in the hot sunshine outside the open dining-hall doors waiting for the lunch queue to go down a bit when I heard the voice behind me. It wasn't the first time I had been mistaken for a newcomer to the jail by somebody who hadn't been here too long himself. It has happened with pleasing frequency lately, nearly every time I have a day in. Usually I'm happy to acknowledge the mistake, laugh it off and explain that actually I'm the con who has been here the longest. It's a response that is almost always greeted with a look of surprise, perhaps a 'Blimey!' or two and then a chat about the merits of the place. But this time the questioner's obvious negative tone caused me to take my time before turning to answer.

I know that somebody in my position can be a valuable source of information to prisoners not long out of the closed system. I can answer a lot of questions, 'How long do we have to go out on community work? When can we start looking for a job? Town visits? Bank account? Car?'

Most of the time I'm happy to share my knowledge. In my early months I was lucky that I knew a couple of people who could put me right on certain matters. Mickey Folsom was the most helpful in the beginning. Wily, hardy, dapper Mickey. He was so pleased to see me when I landed. And though I was wary of hooking up with him to begin with, I can look back now and feel something akin to nostalgia at our early exchanges.

Mickey was eager to tell me about the freedoms we were allowed and the opportunities available. I was all ears. Could everything he was telling me be true? 'It's all up to you,' Mickey said. 'You won't get another chance like this.' Wherever he is now, the fact that he failed so badly in the end will probably be as big a mystery to him as it was to the rest of us.

'Well, what do you think then?' demanded Mr Negative, bringing me back to the present with a jolt. It didn't feel like over two years since Mickey had absconded. After six months on the run the police picked him up as he was about to commit a further serious crime. It was a 'ready eye', meaning the police had been watching and waiting for him to make his move. The last I heard, he got another fifteen years, on top of the twenty he was already doing. Can a life end up any more wasted?

'It's not too bad,' I said, acknowledging Mr Negative at last, 'so long as you use your time here effectively.'

'What the fuck does that mean?' he said.

'Whatever you take it to mean.' I wasn't trying to sound sanctimonious, but that was how I probably came across. It would have been less trouble just to say, 'Yeah, this is OK, as jails go,' obliging Mr Negative with a supportive whinge. Instead I told him how long I'd been here and hoped for some enthusiastic grilling. It never came.

'But it's boring,' he said. 'When I was in [here he named a clutch of well-known closed prisons], at least I knew what I was supposed to be doing. They said I'd get some rehabilitation here...'

'Let me stop you there,' I said. 'What do you mean, "It's boring"? Right now there are more than 75,000 people locked up in prisons across the country. God knows how many thousands are behind their doors for most of the day. There can't be any more than a few hundred with the opportunities we've got here.'

'Listen,' I continued, tapping my temple so firmly it hurt. 'Rehabilitation, or whatever you want to call it, is in here. It's a way of thinking. Open your eyes. Visit the library, the education block, the gym. Think about the poor bastards who are banged up in Wandsworth all day in this heat while you're having your nice after-lunch stroll on the grass and deciding how you're going to spend your afternoon. Chances like this...'

'All right, all right,' he said. 'I'm just saying... it's not as easy as I thought it was going to be.'

'If it was easy,' I said, 'we'd all be going back out "rehabilitated". Nobody's going to spoon-feed it to us. It's something we've got to do for ourselves.'

The look on his face told me what he thought of me, so I wasn't surprised when he declined to join me in the dining hall. But I didn't feel slighted. Who we choose to associate with in prison is as much our own prerogative as the way we choose to do our time.

17 June 2004

Rinty's situation casts a shadow

When I got my release date from the parole board the other week, I had to write and tell my old pals Big Rinty and Felix the Gambler. I knew they would be pleased for me. The Gambler replied straight away. 'Fantastic news,' he wrote, 'but be prepared for the anti-climax.'

Typical advice from the deep-thinking one, though I detected a smidgen of jubilation as he related some positive news about his own situation. 'I've been granted some unaccompanied resettlement leave. Next month. Four days!' I knew he had a paid job in a local recycling plant and that his release was on the horizon, possibly even this year. It was heartening to know that things were going from good to better for the once notorious risk-taker and, after nine years on lifer-recall, not before time. Unlike Rinty's case.

Rinty took a little longer to reply. And it was just a card, a few brief words of congratulation. 'You'll fly once you're out,' he wrote generously. Fair play to the Rint. He explained that he had just finished another offending-behaviour course and had a post-course 'case conference' coming up. 'I'll phone you when I've got some news,' he concluded, adding a PS in capitals, 'DUNDEE FOREVER'.

Rinty is about to start his eighth year in prison following his recall. I know that a life-sentence prisoner can be recalled at any time after release on licence if the authorities feel that the behaviour of the individual in question is giving 'cause for concern'. But I'm struggling to understand how such a long stint of extra imprisonment could be justified when a jury found Rinty not guilty of the allegation that led to his recall in the first place. He was out for three years, after all, and doing well. I know that 'protection of the public' is the paramount consideration in the decision-making process regarding the progress of lifers. But I knew Rinty eighteen years ago.

As cons go, I found him an easy man to get along with.

Nothing unusual stood out – apart from his sense of humour. Sometimes he would make us laugh till we cried. In the transcription workshop where I first met him, he was the 'number one' – a position given only to the most conscientious worker. He was responsible for training up the new men, and taught me. I didn't know much about his case, it's true – but the prison officials did. He had spent years on one-to-ones with psychologists and probation officers until they knew him as well as anyone could.

When he left the high-security system it was because the experts were confident that the risk of further offences was low. After eight years of gradually lowered security, making just over eighteen years in all, Rinty was released. Now that they have more than twenty-five years' knowledge of Rinty, can there be anything else left to find out?

When I answered a call on my mobile phone this week and heard Rinty's voice, I was sure he was ringing with good news. 'So how'd it go?' I asked.

'It was a disaster,' he said. 'They've recommended I do another twelve-month course.'

I couldn't believe it. It got even more puzzling. 'The recommendation has been made without me even having been risk-assessed or having had a treatment-needs assessment. All the reports from the course facilitators are excellent so I don't know what's going on,' he said. During the case conference he had realized that there was a lot of prevarication. Eventually he had asked if he could ask questions. 'Go ahead,' said the chairman.

Rinty took a deep breath. 'Is this another life sentence?'

'No,' said the chairman. 'It's the same one.'

'But how can it be?' asked Rinty. 'You're treating me as if the first eighteen years I did don't count for anything. Has anyone looked at my file for those years?'

'Er, no,' said the chairman. 'We're not sure where it is.'

That was enough to make Rinty's mind up. Outside the room after the conference, one of the prison officers who acts as a facilitator said he would help Rinty by getting him on a course 'by

November'. Rinty gave him a look and replied, 'Fred, there's as much chance of me doing another one of your courses as there is of you and me having a love child.'

I couldn't help laughing at that one, though a part of me wanted to cry. Whatever Rinty did twenty-eight years ago, what is happening to him now just cannot be right.

24 June 2004

Car trouble

It had to happen sooner or later, I guess. Maybe I was being naive, but I was sure it would be later rather than sooner – and in any case, I was certain it wouldn't happen until some time after my release. Like everyone else, I see the fluctuating crime levels reported in the papers every day; and every other week or so, on my travels to and from work, I see boards erected by the police seeking information and witnesses relating to some incident or other: an assault on an elderly person, a hit-and-run driver. In crowded spaces I feel uneasy when individuals are behaving oddly: drink- or drug-fuelled outbursts so often create anxiety among those of us going about our everyday business.

I hoped it wouldn't be a mugging. A physical confrontation could be particularly problematic. No matter what the circumstances, in the aftermath of such an incident I would no doubt be carted back to jail to await the outcome of the inevitable 'internal investigation'.

A pickpocket could also cause me serious problems. That was why I started keeping the licence that permits me to be out and about in my back trouser-pocket rather than my wallet. (Worthless to a thief, but to me the most valuable item on my person.) There was no chance of me getting burgled, not for another few weeks at least. And anyway, joking apart, I believed for some unknown reason that the chances of someone in my situation becoming a crime victim were probably much less than those of the average law-abiding citizen. Which was why I was so unprepared for what I found when I got off the train the other night and went into the car park to collect my old Volvo.

When I saw the stranger looking at my front nearside window, I frowned. He saw me walking towards him and stepped back. There was no reason as far as I could see why anyone should have been paying such close attention to my nondescript motor. As I drew closer, the man turned and climbed into the new-looking metallic blue Mercedes parked alongside my car. He started the engine and lowered his window. It was then I noticed the puddle of broken glass on the floor by my front passenger door.

'It's a mess, I'm afraid,' said the man in the Merc sympathetically. 'Have you got a mobile?' I stared at the black hole where my passenger window should have been and nodded. 'Well, good luck,' he said, before pulling away, leaving me to survey the damage alone. He was right: it was a mess.

It was one of those moments when time seems to stand still. It was nine o'clock at night. I had just done a day's work. I was worn out. Of all the cars in the car park that day, I kept wondering – why mine? Stupid question, really. Like most low-level crime, it was nothing personal. Of all people I should have known that. Whoever had smashed their way in and ripped out the car radio must have been desperate. Good-quality sets are advertised for sale for a few pounds every week in the local paper. Had this been necessary? Obviously it had seemed so to somebody.

Finally I acted. I was loath to call the police, but realized I would have to if I wanted any help from my insurance company. The trouble was, I didn't know what number to call – was it still 999? I pressed the buttons.

'Emergency services,' said the female operator. 'Which service do you require?'

Suddenly I realized two things: first, that it was the first time in my life that I had ever called 999, and second, that I wasn't sure if what had happened to my car could actually be termed an emergency. 'Er, police,' I said.

Seconds later a voice asked me how he could help. I began by apologizing if the crime I was reporting did not appear very serious, but... The policeman interjected, 'We treat all reported crime as serious, sir.' Reassured, I explained what had happened. I couldn't fault the officer for his courtesy. I was transferred through several departments, all of which seemed to be staffed by similarly polite, professional people. By the time I had finished the crime-reporting process, I had been called 'sir' so many times, my self-esteem ended up with a huge and unexpected boost. So much so that the whole thing almost seemed worth it.

Needless to say, I don't expect anyone to be apprehended for what happened. It was unpleasant and inconvenient, but I won't be losing any sleep over it. Neither am I keen for the perpetrator to suffer. Whoever did it must already have a pretty wretched life.

1 July 2004

Too tired for Ricketts

It shouldn't bother me I suppose, but it does feel odd being the con who's been in the prison the longest. Odder still is that there is nobody left in here who I know very well. The only fellow prisoner I now have any kind of a relationship with is Ricketts. He's the only one with whom I feel on relatively friendly terms.

Yet even though he must have been here for at least eighteen months, Ricketts and I have never had a conversation that lasted more than a couple of minutes. I'm not even sure how we became acquainted, although I have a distant recollection that our first encounter occurred as we passed on one of the corridors. Instead of following the usual interaction-avoidance routine (the mumbled 'a'right' and dipped-head technique), Ricketts had beamed me a full-face smile, which I instinctively returned. It was enough for me to take the time to find out his name. Whenever we bumped into each other after that it was like the meeting of two good pals. 'Hey Ricks, how's things?' Instantly we'd both be smiling. 'Excellent, thanks. What about you?'

They were only ever brief exchanges, usually weeks apart: in the meal queue, in the laundry room and, later on, at the gate (one of us coming in, the other going out). We'd share snippets of progress info – neither of us ever failing to be upbeat about the other's prospects. That I knew very little about Ricketts, other than the fact that I liked him, didn't matter at all. Often in prison that is all you really need to know about a fellow body.

But when I answered the knock on my room door the other night and found Ricketts standing there it was a second or two before my face cracked a smile. It was late, nearly ten o'clock, and I was just about to get my head down. 'Ricks,' I said. 'How's it going?'

'Good,' he said, smiling – but it wasn't his usual relaxed beamer either.

'Look,' he said. 'I know you probably don't want the hassle, but there's a guy upstairs who's not long landed and his head's in bits. I think he could do with someone like you to talk to him.'

'Someone like me?' I said. I wasn't sure what that meant. I've been so preoccupied with life outside over the past few weeks that I've hardly noticed what's been going on around me in the jail. On days in I'm mostly in my room working. An agreement when I started my full-time job allows me to 'work from home' on such days.

When I'm working I rarely venture out, except to visit the dining hall and, if the big compound is open, to go out for a run. Otherwise I spend the day surrounded by papers from the office, working on funding applications and other means of developing the organization. The difficulties that fellow cons might be facing rarely take up much of my thinking time these days. I've made my contribution. All I want is for the next stage in my life to begin. If I were a horse I'd be champing at the bit.

'I know we've never talked much,' said Ricketts. 'But since I've been here, whenever I've seen you around you always seem so focused.'

'Well, I...'

'That's how I've tried to do my time,' he said. 'Staying focused.

Using the time. I've got a girl waiting. I want her to be proud of me. When I asked people about you, ages ago, I heard how long you had done and seeing how you did it helped me to put my five-stretch into perspective.'

'Well, that's good,' I said, 'but...'

'The geezer upstairs has only got twenty-three months left, but to him it feels like a lifetime. He says he can't stand being so close to the outside with that amount of bird still to do. He's on about going back into the closed system. I told him about you, about how you do your time. I said he should focus on the positive and not throw away his chance to make this place work for him. Then I wondered if you'd have a word with him.'

'Ricks,' I said, 'I'm sorry but I'm too tired.' He looked disappointed and asked if I'd be around at the weekend. 'I will be,' I said, 'but I'll still be too tired.' I told him my head was more out than in at the moment and that anyway, as far as I could see, he was as likely as anyone to get his neighbour motivated.

After he'd gone I felt a little selfish. It would have cost nothing to have gone along and tried to have a talk with his associate. It sounds like a feeble excuse, I know, but right now, when it comes to engaging with prison life, I genuinely am just too tired.

8 July 2004

Checking my kit

With the weeks rolling by as they have during the past few months I had all but forgotten about my 'stored prop' – the excess stuff that over the years I have had to send to the main prison-service storage depot. It was only after I overheard a reception officer telling a new arrival that the surplus kit he had brought with him would have to be 'sent to Branston', that I was prompted to think about it. (Branston, Staffordshire, is where the depot is located.) I wasn't even sure how many boxes I had in storage. But with my release date looming I knew I had to get an application in quick if I wanted to retrieve them in time.

As I filled in the form I was suddenly tempted to just leave the boxes where they were. After all, there was nothing that I had been missing, nothing that I obviously needed. If I had been pressed I would have struggled to say precisely what any of them contained – which isn't surprising, since I sent the first one away in 1986. By then I had been inside for two years and I was getting rather bogged down with books and other educational materials cluttering up the meagre cell space. Most of the items I had finished with had become so important to me that I had been reluctant to dispose of them permanently. Storage had been the only solution.

'Are you sure they're all mine?' I asked the reception officer. He showed me the paper on his clipboard. 'They've got your name and number on the tags. They match my reference numbers,' he said.

It was a while before I could face opening any of them. For five days they sat stacked in my room like a pile of mysterious time capsules. It was Saturday when I finally got around to checking the contents, and that took me the whole afternoon and most of the night. Each time I lifted a lid I was greeted by a fresh waft of musty air. Books, files, papers. Three radios. A mini gadget for boiling water in a cup (an accompanying note said that it was an 'unauthorized article' and had been confiscated during a cell-search; it didn't ring any bells). There were clothes – including the tie I wore at my trial – and letters, bundles and bundles of letters. It was eerie seeing the writing of family and friends, contact with most of whom had dried up long ago. Some were long dead. There were more books, more papers. It was impossible not to be sidetracked reading old copies of my early prison reports.

By bedtime I was emotionally exhausted. The boxes represented different stages of my life sentence. They were like a chronicle of my life inside and brought the length of time I've been in sharply into focus. In 1986 I had a full head of dark curly hair. That summer I read *The Upstart* by Piers Paul Read, *A Day in the Life of Ivan Denisovich* by Alexander Solzhenitsyn, and *The*

Executioner's Song by Norman Mailer. Holding those books in my hands again brought back powerful memories – memories of huge loss. There was so much to come to terms with then, and there still is, in many ways. But I am now resigned to the fact that I will never have all the answers. The reassuring thing was that after going through the boxes I was left feeling that I had served this sentence in the best way that I could.

But what to do with them now? I considered my options. Only the books were worth a reprieve. But I couldn't hump them around with me for the rest of my life. Maybe I could sell them at a car-boot sale, I thought jokingly. Perhaps there would be a premium on a prisoner's things – on the other hand, perhaps not. In the end I donated the books that were still in good order to the prison library. Everything else went to the incinerator.

22 July 2004

Dilemma at the dentist's

Another new situation, another judgement-call. This time it was a visit to the dentist, which normally wouldn't be a problem, except this was a dentist on the outside and I was trying to decide whether I should reveal to the receptionist that I was still a serving prisoner. I pass the smart chrome-and-glass frontage of the surgery every morning on my walk from the city station to the office, and if it hadn't been for the notice on the door last week I'd never have considered that it might be a place suitable for the likes of me.

'Last few NHS places available,' the notice announced. 'Sign up now.' I wasn't in great need of a dentist, but you never know when an emergency might occur – and I had seen on television news reports the queues caused by the shortage of NHS dentists. It was an opportunity too good to miss.

In the waiting room the receptionist handed me a form to fill in. How stupid I'd been. Of course I couldn't just give my name.

171

They wanted an address, personal details, the name of my doctor. I hesitated before writing in the boxes. The receptionist had called me 'Mr'. Her manner towards me had been impeccably courteous and I didn't want that to change. Knowing my status might not affect her attitude, but how could I be sure?

It's not exactly the same, I know, but I remember when the Kid revealed to some strangers on a train a couple of years ago that he was a prisoner working in the community. He had done his ten years and was on the verge of release. He had worked hard and not wasted any of his prison time – a remarkable feat, considering he was sentenced to life at the age of sixteen. It must have been a daunting prospect in the beginning; it must have seemed undoable. But he did it. And with the outside world beckoning, I understood his need to be accepted for who he was, to be acknowledged as a fellow human being again by ordinary people. I wasn't sure that a crowded train compartment was the right place to test the water, mind you.

He'd got talking, and the big question was inevitable, 'And what do you do?' When it came, the Kid told the truth. 'It just didn't feel right to lie,' he told me afterwards. He got a considerate reaction, but he was lucky – it could easily have ended in tears.

A few weeks ago, when my car was in for repairs after it had been broken into, I managed to get a lift to the station in a fellow prisoner's car. But I had to get a cab for the return trip as I hadn't had time to book a place in the prison van. The driver was female and she smiled when I asked her if she was free. I plonked my briefcase in the back and as I climbed in after it I told her the address of my destination.

'The prison?' she said.

'Er, yes please.'

It felt nice to be chauffeured. I had no intention of letting on to the driver that it was my first unfettered minicab ride in twenty years, nor was I going to mention that those twenty years had been spent in prison. But I hadn't especially intended to keep my prisoner status from her. After all, she knew where I was going.

Then, less than a minute into the journey, she asked, 'Worked there long?' Before I could chuckle and correct her mistake she added, 'If you ask me, I think that lot get too much.' My good mood waned.

We had another fifteen minutes together. I wanted to engage with her, to find out why she had that mean attitude. But there wasn't time. So I let her believe I was a member of staff, asked her to drop me by the works department offices, and gave her a £2 tip. I hated myself for not disclosing the truth, but decided, on balance, it was necessary in the circumstances.

The receptionist at the dentist's, on the other hand, had not mistaken me for anything other than a potential patient. I liked that. It's what I was. I didn't want her to think of me as anything else. So I wrote my soon-to-be home address on the form. Where it asked for doctor's details, I wrote that I hadn't lived there long and hadn't yet registered. The receptionist read through my details and didn't bat an eyelid.

'We have a complimentary clean for new patients. Can I book you an appointment?' She called me 'Mr' again.

'Yes,' I said. 'Thank you. Thank you so much.' I was conscious of sounding overly grateful. She could never have guessed why.

29 July 2004

Twenty years to the day – almost

I've had some long weeks in prison during this sentence, but last week felt like the longest. Even though my days in the office were, as usual, fully occupied, as soon as there was a lull in activity, I couldn't stop myself thinking about the fact that I'm on the verge of getting out. Each time, I was hit by a fresh rush of adrenaline. I kept having to push my chair away from the desk for a few moments just to catch my breath. The train journeys to and from the city seemed to take longer too, especially the ones taking me back to prison at night. I tried going to bed as soon as I was behind my door – big mistake. Fitful sleep made the nights twice as long.

I tried staying up late, reading, listening to the radio, reading some more, watching my portable television, but it made no difference. The only time it felt like I had managed to get any real sleep was around half an hour before my alarm clock would start squealing at 5.24am. Then it took strength I never knew I had to drag myself out from under the covers and along the corridor to the shower room. In the mirror above the sinks, my eyes had never looked blearier. I thought the week would never end. But it has. And now I'm down to my last few days.

I haven't talked about it to many people in the jail. The pals who I would have shared these feelings with – the Poet, Tank, the Kid – all went to better lives long since. I wrote my last letter from prison to Big Rinty the other week, just to let him know he wasn't forgotten. He replied and said he was proud of me. 'Give it your best shot out there. There'll be no more chances.'

People in the jail must have been talking. Twice this week, while waiting in the outside-workers' queue for the gate to be opened, I was asked by fellow cons, 'You're out soon aren't you?' Each time I answered with a simple 'Yes.' I knew they wanted more information. I didn't want to appear unwilling to engage, but neither did I particularly want to talk about it. The truth is, I can hardly believe that it is actually going to happen. Discussing it makes me nervous. I know the date I've been given. It corresponds with the day that marks twenty years exactly since I was taken into custody.

When I went to get 'fitted for release' by the nurse in healthcare the other day, she asked me when I was out. I said, 'Er, next week, I think.'

She smiled and gave me a puzzled look. 'You think? Don't you know?'

'Well, I think I know,' I said, and she burst out laughing. The trouble was, I wasn't joking. Is it really true? Am I really going home at last? The nurse said she was pleased to sign the slip saying that I had been checked over and could confirm that there was no medical reason why I should not be discharged.

Stepping out of healthcare into the hazy, muggy sunshine, I almost wept with relief – relief that I had not wasted my time inside. Once, in the early days, when I was trying to figure out how I was going to do this thing, I decided it was important that I try to follow as healthy a lifestyle as I could. It might be possible, I mused, to live in such a way that the back end of my life might be extended to make up for the time I was going to lose. There's no way of knowing if, by keeping fit and using my brain, I have made extra years of living possible – though I doubt I would have lived even this long if I hadn't come to prison when I did.

One thing I do know is that in prison I have created a new life – a life worth living. I look back at the young man who began this sentence twenty years ago and sometimes I find it hard to connect with him. When I stood in front of the judge and took my life imprisonment I was about as broken and defeated as a man could be. Rebuilding was a big task, but with some helping hands along the way, and steel-hard determination, I've done it. I can't change the past – I would sacrifice all my good things if I could – but I've managed to change me. It was the best that I could do.

5 August 2004

Acknowledgements:

Thank you to Toby, Alice and Louisa of Atlantic Books and Lisa of Guardian Books for all your goodwill. And to the many Guardian readers who were open hearted enough to send me encouraging cards and letters as I served the last four and a half years of my life inside. Your support was appreciated more than words can say. Thank you every one. Finally, to Ronan Bennett who opened the door of opportunity that led to my parallel life as a Guardian columnist in the first place. Your friendship brought colour into what had become colourless days. You were and continue to be a peerless role model. Thank you.